SNAKE

CONFESSIONS OF A REPLACEMENT ROCK STAR

STACEY BLADES

© Copyright 2009.

I often wonder if we create our own forces in the universe and I'm sure everybody has had their own pattern of "Snake Eyes" in their life. I really feel for me that I lived it, ate it, breathed it and still do. There was something I always felt as a kid; that certain unknown of "what's around the corner feeling" and still do to this day. I've certainly experienced some nerve wracking shit in my life. I have a feeling that it was all to make me a stronger person or a serious test to challenge my devotion to music. Writing this book has been very therapeutic and I felt it was necessary to share some much needed knowledge about my name, my career and my life. I hope you enjoy it as much as I enjoyed writing it.

- STACEY BLADES-

ACKNOWLEDGMENTS

I would like to thank God first and foremost for being by my side for every victory, loss, screw-up, let down, heartbreak and accomplishment. Thank you for believing in me!

Thank you very much to my friends and band mates for letting me hound them for confessionals. Thanks be to Lisa Grollino, Mom and Dad, Phil Lewis, Junko Lewis, Steve Riley, Mary Louis Riley, Scotty Griffin, The Campbell Family, Adam Hamilton, Mike Duda, Joey Allen, Lee Markel, Frank Kenny, Brian Majencic, Anthony Bozza, Bruce Clark, Eric Stacey, Vikk Foxx, Lantz L'amour, Jamie Zimlin, Jon Levin, Tyson Cornell, Carolyn Haskell, Rudy Sarzo, Denise Ames, Andy and Annette Johns, Aaron Barrocas, Bobby Blotzer, Heidi Horvath, and Brooke Mckaig.

Special thanks to Scott Mckenzie for all your help and support on the book.

A special thanks to all the fans worldwide for your love and support.

PHOTO CREDITS

Jenn, Ron Boudreau, D.W., Mark Walentiny, Andrew Orth, Cherie Boyle, Junko Lewis, Heidi Horvath, Suzanne Fouliard and various friends and family whose snapshots over the years came in handy for use in this book.
Cover artwork and layout by Brooke Mckaig.

PROLOGUE:

August 18th, Hollywood, CA. L.A. Guns is playing at a new venue called the Vine St. Lounge. Really cool new place. So we launch into the set and we really fog the place up. Next thing we know the fogger sets off the fire alarm. 118 decibels of blasting shrieks, which lasts the whole set. Shit, the Fire Department showed up and couldn't even shut that fucker down. I really believe there are forces in the world of rock and roll that constantly fuck with your game. In this book you will find out that I was certainly the poster child for this notion and my life.

TABLE OF CONTENTS

CHAPTER 1.... WELCOME TO THE WORLD

CHAPTER 2..... REBEL WITH A CAUSE

CHAPTER 3..... STARS IN HIS EYES

CHAPTER 4......SOUTH OF THE BORDER

CHAPTER 5..... IT'S A JUNGLE OUT THERE

CHAPTER 6...... ILLUSIONS OF GRANDUER

CHAPTER 7......MISERY LOVES COMPANY

CHAPTER 8.....THE CITY OF ANGELS

CHAPTER 9 ....STACEY GET YOUR GUN

CHAPTER 10....A NEW BEGINNING

CHAPTER 11...DOWN UNDER

CHAPTER 12....IN THE MIX

CHAPTER 13... .ALL ROADS LEAD HERE

WELCOME TO THE WORLD

CHAPTER 1

Let the show begin. The year is 1968. My birth parents, what little I know of them, were attending University in Calgary, Alberta Canada. I want to believe they were in love but the truth of the matter is they were probably just knocking boots which ended with my birth mother being knocked up with me! I really believe that her family told her to give up her child. My adoptive mother told me that when they signed the adoption papers, under no circumstances whatsoever was my birth mother to be contacted, ever! I think she was only in her early 20's. I was born on November 4th. That means I must have been conceived in February, probably in a dorm room or something. I was born Brian and that's all I know. One week later I was adopted by Peter and Shirley Ingram, the only parents who I would know and love. However I would spend a lifetime wondering just who the fuck I was. I guess it was some kind of separation anxiety, you know- where am I from? Where do I get my looks from? What's my ancestry?

When I was born there were a few complications. When I popped out, my right leg was somehow twisted to the left. That means they had to break it and reform it straight. I was convinced in my later years that my birth mom was a hippie. (I still believe she smoked pot) I spent the first 3 years of my life in and out of the hospital. I remember this little blue suit I would wear when my mom would pick me up from the hospital. Gee where to start:

When I was 2 years old I had double pneumonia in both my lungs and a temperature of 103. How I didn't die is beyond me. They would dip me in ice baths to break my fever. I was told that they were trying to stick me with a needle but it wouldn't take. I think they tried pricking me over fifty times. I eventually got better; dodged the bullet on that one. A year later my sister and I were playing in our basement of our house in Calgary and she hands me a plastic ball and says it's a "munchie ball." So I popped it in my mouth and gulp! It's an absolute miracle I didn't choke on that thing. Rushed off to the hospital again to get that thing pumped out of my stomach. Dodged the bullet again. My sister was 4 years older than me and also adopted. Her adoption issues would plague her worse than me!

One of my first words that I used to say all the time was "Thanan." Thanan this and thanan that. What the hell was thanan? It's funny how your brain retains stuff from your childhood. I clearly remember pointing at a plane in the sky when I was about 2 and saying "THANAN." My parents were very giving and loving but also ruled us with an iron fist! I wish more parents did this with their kids. You didn't get away with much in my household. However that doesn't mean we didn't occasionally cause trouble. There was nothing they wouldn't give us or take us and we fuckin tortured them for years with unruly behavior, constant screw ups and rebellion which created a very volatile mixture. My mom wanted these perfect angels, wishful thinking right. She so wanted her son to be the perfect suit and tie guy with short hair but got this black haired, tattooed, wild man. The more she tried to change me, the more I rebelled until I was told to leave. Okay I'm jumping ahead a little here.

Skiing with parents---Banff Alberta 1975

mom was pretty much a housewife; she would work from time to time as a secretary and later worked for a company called the Paper Workers Union. My dad worked for Simmons Mattress's for 40 years and retired V.P 12 years ago.

With my newly healing straight leg, I had to wear a brace that was attached to the crib. I also had to wear these interlocking boots so that my foot and ankle healed properly. I was a babysitter's worst nightmare! I must have hated that brace because I would bang my head against the crib. My dad called me a headbanger, little did he know I would turn into one. When I was about 1 or so my Dad would put me on top of the kitchen table and I would dance like a madman! I was already ready to rock I guess.

Shirley Ingram: Stacey's Mom
From the time Stacey was a baby, as soon as he heard music he would start to dance - as a tiny baby, his dad would hold him up on the dining table and his legs would go a mile a minute, smiling the whole time. Stacey has always been single minded which at times can represent itself as stubborn. A few incidents come to mind:

The Sunday he insisted on wearing one of his father's ties to church even though it hung down to his knees (remember, he was only four) but even then when his mind was made up he shut the door on any suggestions to change.

His winter shoveling job for which he was paid in advance was for the McIlroys who lived around the corner from us. Stacey loved being paid but hated the sight of snow falling. His dad would remind him of his commitment and send him off to do the job, one, two, three, maybe four times before it was done to his dad's satisfaction. In the end Stacey managed to talk his dad into seeing the job was done to perfection, showing his management skills at an early age! His answer was, "They won't know if it is a perfect job, they're in Florida for the winter!"
He has always marched, or played, to his own tune.

I was a good kid but a little shit who needed to be smacked once in a while. If I didn't get my way I would usually spazz which led to a wooden spoon across my ass! I had a few friends and one best friend named Mike Bentley. The two of us were quite a pair of little hooligans. We would cruise around in our neighborhood in jean jackets, bell bottoms and cowboy boots. We had these candy cigarettes that we pretended to smoke. Popeye Cigarettes, I think they were called. I remember vaguely one time with Mike loading rocks into my basement. When my mother saw what we were doing she promptly told us to "get all these rocks out of the house now!" Mike simply told me to tell my mother to "fuckoff" which I complied. The two of us I'm sure got our asses beat!

Mostly, I really enjoyed occupying my playtime by myself. I was a strange kid and a control freak. If my friends weren't playing a game right, like cops and robbers, I would flip out and start going off on them. Where the fuck was this behavior coming from? Was I already lashing out at my abandonment by my birth mom?

My parents took my sister and I to California to spend a week at Disneyland. It was our first real vacation with my parents. I remember one afternoon we were all lounging by the pool. I thought I would be brave and tackle the deep end, since my sister had already mastered it. So I got on the pool slide and it flung me into the deep end like a sling shot. I freaked and started to grab onto my sister. Little did I know but I was practically drowning her. My mom finally snapped at my dad, "Would you get in there and get those two before they drown!"

Christmas was always my favorite. My mom would make the most amazing Christmas cookies and she would always have to hide them because we gorged ourselves on them. One Christmas my parents got me the Krank Evel Kinevel motorcycle. Basically it was an action figure of him on a toy bike that you would lock into this windup ramp. You would rev and rev it with a handle and press this button and the thing would shoot out of the ramp at Mach 1. So I revved her up and let Kinevel go and it made a beeline right for the Christmas tree and hit it with such force that it completely knocked the tree down. We would also spend a few Christmas's at Banff Hot Springs. I remember we would roll around in the snow and then jump into the hot tubs.

Every summer we would rent a chalet at this amazing resort spot in Penticton, British Colombia called Ponderosa Point. It was absolutely beautiful there. There were huge pine trees everywhere and green grass and sand. I have fond memories of waking up in the morning to the sound of a nearby train. My sister and I would collect pop bottle caps and place them on the train track so they would get flattened. Yeah, two kids playing by the train tracks, that's safe. The beach was gorgeous and the lake was pristine. It took forever to get there from Calgary and I would drive my parents nuts the whole way there. I used to rock back and forth in the backseat of my dad's car murmuring, "Are we there yet?"

One of our usual staples as a family was going to the local drive-in movie theater to see the latest movies. If you grew up in the seventies, going to the drive-in movies ruled!! There was just something so cool about it. In '74 we ventured out to the drive-in to see "*Jaws*." My parents thought nothing of taking a 6- year to see a movie about a man eating shark terrorizing a seaside town. That fuckin movie traumatized me! I can only imagine the look on my face as that great white spent most of the movie devouring people. However after that movie I became obsessed with sharks. I knew everything and anything about them. I did however have a hard time getting anywhere near a body of water for a long time.

School Photo 1975

I loved music. Anything that I would hear on the radio had such a lasting impression on me. I loved the Bay City Rollers "*Saturday Night*" and Gordon Lightfoot's "*Sundown*." I was always walking around singing songs in my head. I also loved to watch the Sonny and Cher show, which always had some music in it.

In '76 my dad was transferred to Toronto. We sold our house and off we went. I was only 7 at the time, so it didn't bother me too much but it did feel a little strange to leave this familiar abode.

So here we are in Toronto, new neighborhood, new house and I don't know a soul. There were lots of kids who lived on the street and I was starting a new school at the end of summer. We had these neighbors right next to us called the Goridika's. They were this elderly Polish couple and Mr. Gordika was the biggest snoop I have ever seen. As soon as we got to our new house he was immediately showing us every corner of "OUR" house. All I could think was "Who is the whacky old guy?" Here's a few things about ole snoopy Gordika. The time my mother caught him rummaging through our garbage cans at night. My mom seeing Mr. Goridika snooping around our backyard in the middle of the night. The time I walked out of the house and saw Mr. Gordika sitting right in the front seat of my mom's new car! What a strange man he was and he looked like Colonel Sanders.

In third grade, I refused to use scissors for some bizarre reason. This kid nicknamed me Blades and it just stuck! Grade school was okay. I was an active kid who loved sports and made lots of friends. I clearly remember my fifth grade teacher Mrs. Tierney. She was a fuckin bitch and had it in for me from day one. She would pick a student every year and torment them. She used to degrade and humiliate me on a weekly basis. My mom actually went down to the school and went off on her. Mrs. Tierney was pregnant at the time and my mom actually told her "I hope your kid has a teacher like you one day!" This in turn made Mrs. Tierney actually cry. Alright mom!

About a year before we moved to Toronto, my parents friends sons Phillip MckSkimming and Ross Weaver came to live with us. I loved those guys; they were probably in their early 20's and were attending University in Calgary. They were like the brothers I never had. Anyways in the summer of '78 my dad had rented this kickass chalet on Georgian Bay about an hour outside of Toronto in Collingwood. It was a beautiful summer home all made out of wood and had these spectacular bedrooms. Across the street was this private pristine beach cove with white sand and these massive rocks off to the side of the beach that jutted out into the water that you could suntan on. I just remember you could walk out about a hundred yards into the water and you would be only waist deep. In Collingwood they had a ski hill and that particular summer they built this thing called the "Slide Ride." Ross and Phillip were in Toronto for a few weeks and came up to the cottage with us. We had all decided to go into Collingwood and be the first people on the "slide ride," shit they were still kind of doing construction on it. By the time we got to the top of the hill a nasty thunderstorm started brewing. It started pissing rain and then started to hail! There was this little shed with a bunch of wooden sheets around it. There were about 11 of us and we all scrambled under this thing. My dad and a few other gentlemen grabbed those wooden sheets and we made our own protective shed from the hail storm. Now, this shed all of the sudden became the highest point on top of Blue Mountain, you can see where this is going. All of the sudden we see a big flash of white light. A massive bolt of lightning lit our little shed up like a 100 watt light bulb. My dad was holding one of the walls up. The electricity passed through my dad, me, my sister, my mom, Phillip, Ross and 4 other people. I remember my dad and my sister were freaking cause' I think they got the brunt of it. The wooden planks were laced with metal and became an electrical magnet. It finally stopped raining and the staff members of the facility dried the track off and we jetted down the 2 miles of concrete track on our plastic rockets.

    The following year I became friends at the time with this kid named Jonathan. He was the new kid in class and we hit it off. I went over to his house, walked in his room and was like 'Holy Shit' his room was the fuckin coolest thing I had ever seen in my life. He had 6 foot KISS posters everywhere and the coolest toy models I have ever seen. He definitely got me into KISS, shit we even dressed up like them one day. I remember his dad made us wooden guitars with his buzz saw. I would stand in front of the mirror in my room and rock that fucker. By the time I was 10 I really started getting into Rock 'n Roll. You know the typical, Stones, Aerosmith, Rush, The Cars, Cheap Trick and for some reason I liked Styx.

    My family was very musical, (thank God) my mom played piano very well and my sister had already been playing since she was 6. My great uncle was an amazing player. He was like

Liberace and dressed the part too! He was amazing and I loved watching him tinkle the ivories and yes he might have been gay. So my mom decides, let's get you into lessons. I friggin hated it but enjoyed being able to learn how to play music. Fuck, what kid wanted to take piano lessons at age 9? My teacher had this house that smelt weird and she had these creepy long thumbs. She would show me scales and I would just stare at her thumbs. The teachers would setup recitals and it was hard work. If you screwed up you felt like a loser because all these parent's eyes were bearing down on you.

At age 11 my parents bought me a crappy acoustic for Christmas, finally a guitar! I just remember picking it up and banging the strings like no tomorrow. My parents started me with lessons. I went to this old, boring windbag who showed me how to play "Mary had a little lamb" it sucked, trust me. When I was waiting for my lesson one time there was this older kid taking lessons. I clearly remember that this kid asked the teacher if he could learn how to play a Triumph song and the old windbag sternly told him NO! I thought to myself "Fuck this guy I'm outta here." I wanted to learn how to play rock music, not nursery rhymes. I complained to my mom and she found this music store that taught. Seagully Sound I think it was. It was a great place, and filled with all kinds of amps and electric guitars. I remember the first time I went in there and one of the teachers was ripping on this maple blonde Strat and I was just floored. I thought "That's gonna be me in a few years!" I loved going there every week. They would teach me songs. Within weeks I was playing Eagles, Rod Stewart and Rolling Stones. My teacher Mark at the time was floored how well I had gotten over the first three or four lessons. I felt sooo at home there that I just became one with my guitar. Pretty good feeling for being 12.

Getting back to my neighborhood, we lived in a pretty well to do area and it was very "Leave it to Beaver"- ish. All that changed one Sunday morning. As we loaded up in my dad's car on our way to church, we drove up towards the end of the street and there were police cars everywhere and the street was completely barricaded. We soon learned there had been a mass murder that took place in the early morning. At the top of our street lived the Kinnear's. They had three boys and the youngest went to high school with my sister. It turns out that their stepfather, who was a well to do dentist, completely snapped and went into the house that morning with a shotgun and blew the boys away and their mother. One of the middle sons managed to climb out a window, but was cut down as he ran passed their swimming pool. For some reason he didn't kill the Kinnear's grandmother though. I guess after his rampage he went to his first wife's gravestone and blew his head off. Everyone on the street was in utter shock and shit like this only happened in the movies as far as we were concerned. I'll never forget that morning.

Later that year I went to my first concert—Tom Petty and the Heartbreakers. I can't believe that my parents let me and my friend go alone! That next year I wanted to go see Ozzy and my mom totally forbid me. Maybe she felt like she screwed up for letting me go to that Tom Petty show all by myself.

My sister and I were very fortunate. My parents would usually take us on vacation with them. We had gone to the Barbados, Hawaii and the Bahamas. The Hawaii trip was amazing. I think it was around '79. We went with our family friends the St. John's to the Island of Maui for two weeks. The St. John's had a daughter the same age as me, Kathy was her name and I was crazy about her. I would say she was my first real crush and my first real make out session. Kathy and I would chase each other around the hotel and beach and we would ride the elevator up and down while making out. I still to this day have fond memories of that trip and am dying to go back to Hawaii.

Anyways getting back to music, around 13, I discovered Randy Rhoads. He was the first guitarist that changed me chemically (if that makes any sense). I loved lots of other guitar players over the years, Page, Hendrix, Perry, but nobody changed me like Rhoads did. *Diary of a Madman* fuckin ruled as a guitar album. It still to this day makes the hair on my neck stand up.

I got my first electric guitar around the age of 14. It was an old Ibanez Cherry Sunburst Les Paul Copy. It was a '53 deluxe and had the old Ibanez insignia on it. I found it at this guitar store called Ring Music. I can clearly remember taking the subway downtown to get the guitar. It was summer and I was so excited, it felt like I was being charged with electricity. It was a great guitar but the pickups used to howl like a muthafucker when you cranked up the amp. I used to stand in front of the mirror envisioning playing in front of screaming fans with the lights blaring down on me.

I started jamming for the first time around 14 or 15, with this drummer and another guitar player. We were awful but I loved going there and plugging in and playing alongside the drummer, who was actually pretty good. I used to drive these guys nuts because all I wanted to do was play and they were too busy smoking weed and drinking beer. Of course I indulged a few times myself. It was the first time I tried pot, it felt like my head was like a giant balloon.

I used to spend hours in my room listening to the radio while thumbing through travel brochure magazines for tropical destinations. I'd be listening to Judas Priest while reading resort specs for Acapulco, Mexico or something. Funny, how I combined hard rock and tropical locations. What's even funnier, is that I made those two things a reality by playing hard rock in a tropical climate of South Florida. I guess my channeling worked.

I had started high school in '83 and I fuckin hated it! I still hadn't hit puberty and I was a little shrimp. I of course got picked on all the time. I really withdrew and wasn't doing well in school. My parents decided to send my ass to a child psychologist. I hated going there. I remember the doctor asked me what I wanted to do with my life and I said "I'm gonna be a rock star!" He quipped back "Well kid that's a pipe dream." I hated that guy already. After that summer my parents decided to send me to this private school called Thorton Hall. I had to wear the typical suit everyday and had to take the subway uptown everyday which was a pain in the ass.

Shirley Ingram:
Stacey attended a private school in Toronto for one year and was required to wear a school uniform much to his disgust. He was told at the beginning of the year by the Headmaster he MUST always arrive at school with his uniform on. Well that didn't sit too well with Stacey so he would stop in the subway washroom, do a quick change, hop on the subway looking cool in his ripped jeans etc. After a stiff reprimand from Dr. MacKay he begrudgingly turned up at school in his uniform - I often wonder where he changed, closer to the school?

The school was co-ed and they had this amazing art program there. It really wasn't a bad place but they were strict as hell. The Madam Miss Greg ruled that place with an iron fist! If you didn't do your homework you were sent from your classroom into hers and it was announced in front of her and her class that you didn't do your homework. Miss Greg would then berate you in front of everybody and make you feel like a complete jackass! Not only that but they would send your ass home for the day. I remember riding the subway all day because I knew if I went home I would have gotten busted.

Now by this time it was turning around '84 and the first wave of L.A. Metal was starting to hit. I lost my mind when I started hearing all these killer new bands like Motley, Ratt, Rough Cutt, WASP and Dokken. This shit just sucked me into a vortex of sound, and the image was everything I wanted to be. My buddy Rob Peaker and I would walk around the affluent neighborhood we lived in blasting Ratt and Motley on his boombox slugging straight Gin from the bottle. God I felt so alive and this new hard rock took me to places I thought weren't imaginable. Rob and I were total metalheads and we would get together and slug down gin while we blasted Dokken's "*Tooth and Nail.*" Why we choose to drink gin was beyond me. I think he used to lift it from his dad's liquor cabinet. I still can't even smell Gin today without wincing. I remember we got really drunk one night and the next day I had to deliver the Bible reading in front of the whole congregation at the church I went to. My parents were out of town and it was summer. I had to walk all the way to church in the blazing morning sun in a suit. I was so hung over and puked a few times along the way. After I delivered a few psalms from the Bible, I had to duck out of the pew and run to the bathroom to throw up. I didn't quite make it and puked all over the bathroom door and sprayed my shoes at the same time. The good Lord above must have just been shaking his head the whole time at me.

    I also hung out with this lunatic named Trevor Holmes. Trevor and I were tight as hell. Trevor was a straight laced looking jock type but really should have been a rock star 'cause he was nuts. His sense of unbridled adventure always landed us in trouble. His father was British, he reminded me a lot of John Hillerman who played Higgins on *Magnum P.I.* He was very stern with Trevor and his brother that's probably why they were both wild. Trevor and I went to our first metal concert. It was Dio, Helix and Rough Cutt. God that show rocked, 20,000 people at CNE Stadium.

One night Trevor and I were downing tall boys over at his house. His parents were away and his dad had just got this new car. Trevor gets the bright idea to take it for a joy ride. I was very unsure and of course he made me drive. I don't remember what kind of car it was but it was a turbo something and it hauled ass. As we were burning through the neighborhoods, there was a cop car camped out waiting for speeding idiots like ourselves. When I gunned it back on the main road, I saw the flashing lights in back of me. Oh shit!!! I pulled over and the cop came over to the window. Of course I didn't know where anything was in the car and couldn't get the window down to save my life. Once I got the window down, the cop told me to get out of the car. As I was opening the door, I must have locked it and couldn't find the lock and had to open the door from the outside. That looked really good! The officer of course put Trevor and I in the back of the squad car. The cops were total assholes. They let Trevor out and kept me in the backseat. Trevor kept signaling me to "Let's run for it!" I kept looking at him like "are you nuts!" They let me out of the car and confiscated my license for 12 hours and then towed the car. Trevor and I had to walk about six miles home and all we could think about was how bad his dad was going to flip on both of us. Trevor and his brother managed to get the car out of the impound before their parents got back and they never found out. Trevor was totally into the Marines and military, shit he even had a subscription to *"Soldier of Fortune"* magazine. Trevor had even purchased a fuckin M-16 machine gun! He actually kept it in his closet with a fully loaded clip! I remember the time his brother Pat picked up the gun and shot a hole in the wall. Those two are lucky they didn't kill each other. I lost touch with Trevor around '91. I wonder what ever happened to him?

So I knew I was going to be a rock star right! Well I needed a rock star name. Being that my nickname was Blades, that was a given. But what to put in front of that? One of my favorite movies was *"Up in Smoke"* with Cheech and Chong. I thought Stacy Keach was brilliant in that movie. He had the coolest name too. BING, light bulb goes off...... Stacey Blades! Man I thought it ruled! (Of course in later years when I joined L.A. Guns I would get ripped on the internet by the typical gossip board douche bag losers claiming I stole the name from Tracii Guns). Of course nobody ever said anything about that the whole eight years I was in Roxx Gang. I forgot to mention I was totally in love for the first time. Her name was Cheryl Duke, she was tall, blonde and beautiful and she was the spitting image of Daryl Hannah. She meant the world to me and I met her at a youth group meeting. It was full blown love at first sight. I staked my claim on her right away.

Anyways, I started a new high school and felt really comfortable there. I hooked up with this Italian dude named Mike Zingone, who was a good guitar player. We also recruited this kid Jamie who was a wiz on keyboards. Mike knew this drummer Eric who was a year older than us and in the next grade. I had heard of Eric and knew he was a badass. We jammed on lots of covers and had a few good originals. Mike, Jamie and I would split the singing on the songs. I can't quite remember who the bass player was? My first gig with these guys was at my high school Star Search Night. The auditorium was packed with 750 kids. I walked out on stage and fuckin shit!! The crowd seemed to like us though and I lost my stage fright quick. I knew this is where I wanted to be!

Summer 1987

I wore a tight jean jacket with jeans and beige Capezzios and my hair spiked to the guilds with my Les Paul. I thought I was the shit! This band of course ended up kicking me out because I wanted to rock and all they wanted to do is play top 40 songs. I was pissed and said, "I'll start a kick ass metal band, who needs you guys, fuckin later!!"

REBEL WITH A CAUSE

CHAPTER 2

I knew this kid named Dean; he was a year younger than me and in the grade below me. He was a kickass drummer for his age and had killer long, streaked hair. I said I wanted to start a band like Motley and Ratt which was right up his alley. He also was friends with this rocker kid Brent who could fuckin play guitar like a pro! So we started jamming and started writing some amazing stuff in the vein of all these new metal bands. Dean also knew this kid who lived down the street who played bass. He had long blonde hair and had his own P.A. system. Fuck, could this kid play. He was 16 and could pull off Billy Sheehan licks. Nobody could hold a candle to us for a band that was this young. We were on fire and writing songs that were radio ready! We just couldn't find a good singer. We settled on this dirt bag named Glen who couldn't sing all that well but got the job done. The band finally started to play gigs in bars. The first shithole we played was fuckin packed and my legs felt like spaghetti. Everyone in that place was floored at how good we were! I was convinced that we were going to make it after that night. If we would have had a killer singer, we probably would have. The timing was perfect. It was the beginning of 1987 and our look was great. We had managers and agents offering their help. I was so green and stupid; I guess we all were, that we fucked it up! This manager guy kept saying "Sack this singer, he sucks, I can get you guys a tour in Canada but you've got to get someone new." The bass player already quit because of this singer and it all started to fall apart. Plus we couldn't find someone to replace him. Brent then followed suit and quit. Well here we go again. I'm destined to follow this chain of events: A sure fire star that never fired. (Well eventually). I think if Blind Desire (name of the band) wasn't so young and naïve we could have had a chance to make it. Too bad, we fuckin burned and slayed the audience every time we played.

Live Shot '88- Blind Desire

Getting back to Cheryl, we did everything together! She was my drug and the sex was incredible. I loved her so much and would have taken on a raging bull for her but at the same time my fucked up warped sense of reality would show. I would test her and put her through hell. I would call her up and say something stupid like "I'm really no good for you and we should breakup!" This would of course send her into sobbing tears and I would just snicker on the other end of the phone. What the hell was wrong with me! She was the best thing that ever happened to me.

My parents started to go away a lot and would be gone sometimes for three weeks at a time, especially in the summer. My sister was working at a resort that summer and I remember she came home to get my dad's car. I thought "Oh boy, this is not a good idea." I told my sister not to take my dad's car but she just laughed and grabbed the keys. Off she went. A week later I was walking out of the house and here's this tow truck pulling up to the driveway with my dad's Thunderbird in tow and my sister sitting in the front seat of tow truck. "What the hell did you do?" "I don't know, it just stopped running." I can only imagine what my sister did to that car. I wasn't exactly innocent myself. My mom had left me her car keys and said I could use her car but only to run errands and go over to my friends. Of course I took her car up to Wasaga Beach which was an hour and half outside of Toronto with Cheryl, Dean and Brent. I guess the brake pads on her Mazda must have started to go bad because by the end of those three weeks the brakes were grinding like a son of a bitch.

Of course that didn't stop me from driving. When my parents came home I didn't say shit. My mom needed to go somewhere and got in her car and started to back out of the driveway and SCREEEEEECH! Busted! Then she grabs my dad's keys and gets in the Thunderbird and Uhguhguhguhguhguhguhgu……. My mom got out of the car and was double pissed!!

"What the hell did you do to my brakes and why is your father's car not starting!" I had to come clean. My mom told me I was never going to drive her car again. She really must have meant it because I never did again!

I had these two friends at the time named Jeremy and Andrew Elijosis who we just called Eli. I thought I liked drinking beer, but these two were the "Jedi Masters" of ale. Hell they both even brewed their own beer in their parent's basement! Eli and Jeremy would go out and get so rotted that they would end up falling asleep on the subway. Their usual routine was that they would hit a couple of places downtown and then after the bars would close, head home on the subway. They of course would pass out and miss their stop at the end of the west end of the city. The subway would then go back the opposite way and they would wake up somewhere east of downtown about 25 stops past their original station. They would be totally screwed because it was the last train heading east for the night.

One time I had Eli, his girlfriend and Cheryl over to my place. My parents had gone out for the evening and Eli and his chick had decided to venture into my bedroom while Cheryl and I hung in my basement. As I was lying on the couch with Cheryl, I see my dad walking down the stairs. I guess they had decided to come home a little early, much to my surprise. My dad was like "what the hell is going on?" When my parents got home, I guess my dad walked into my room while Eli and his chick were getting busy. Eli had all the lights off and thought it was me coming into the room. He muttered out "One second Chief." I guess he realized it wasn't me when he saw the back of my dad with his suit walking out of my room. I went upstairs into my room and the both of them looked like they had seen a ghost! I told them "You best be going." I don't think Eli called my house for months after that. My dad thought the whole thing was funny but my mom was pissed.

   I graduated high school at the end of spring '87. That was one of the best years of my life actually. I had made a ton of new friends by that year and really enjoyed going to school, I mean somewhat. That last year was a breeze. They had switched the program that year of how your classes were laid out. They had this two day cycle. The first day I had five classes; then on day two, I only had one or two classes I think. They were both in the morning so I would be done by lunch and split home. It was great.

   My buddies and I really got into smoking weed that year. We had these Friday night gatherings over at my friend Andrew's apartment. We called it "Floyd Night." We would take all the light bulbs out of every lamp and replace them with blue lights and then put on Pink Floyd's "*Dark Side of the Moon*" or "*The Wall*" and just smoke out. One time we had gone to this nasty housing project to buy sensimilla and we were all going to get together over at my buddy's place. We were all jammed into a tent smoking this crap we bought. Little did I know it was laced with LSD or something. After about an hour or so we were downstairs all sitting around completely stoned listening to some weird new wave version of "Money, That's What I want" and I started really tripping. All of the sudden all my friends kind of merged into "Jabba the Hut" from *Star Wars*. He just sat there laughing at me till I stood up and shook my head. My friend Matt was on the floor in the fetal position hallucinating that he could move his hands and arms through his stomach. I hated the way I felt and was tripping my balls out. I just had to ride it out. Some people like hallucinating or tripping, but I hated it!

I played in the school jazz band the last 2 years of high school. We were renowned and were the best in the city and were able to travel all over the world. The band and the orchestra was run by Music Director Don Strathdee. Mr. Strathdee really took a liking to me. I think he saw that spark in my eye. He took me under his wing and sculpted me into a disciplined musician. Don would push me and other musicians and bring the best out in us. He was a great guy but a ball buster too. He was usually a lot of fun on those band trips and usually partied with us, pretty cool considering the guy was in his early 50's! That year we traveled to Puerto Vallarta, Mexico. We were there for seven days and only had two shows to play. We had so much fun. All my high school buddies were also in the band. We would just lie on the beach, knock back Coronas and go to clubs. I have fond memories of smoking pot pool side at three in the morning. I had everybody wetting themselves as I was busting out all these ridiculous riddles. One night we had this guy with a bus taking us all over to these different clubs. Strathdee and the rest of the chaperones went out for the night as well. We were heading back to the hotel and everybody was kind of buzzed. I look out the window of the bus and there's Strathdee's car right next to us! He looked like he was panning over all of us and could tell we were up to no good. Strathdee had a sixth sense and would always know when we were misbehaving. He of course decided to do a room check that night. Well earlier that night we had met this couple from L.A. who had won a weekend to Mexico on the "*Dating Game Show*." We started to party with them and they decided to come back with us to the hotel. Of course here comes the knock on the door. "Open up the door it's Strathdee!" I yell "Hide!" The chick and the guy kneeled on the floor and put a blanket over them. It was fuckin hilarious but Strathdee was pissed. He told the chick to put on her walking shoes and get the hell outta here! Don died of a brain tumor a year after I graduated. The man was a mentor and I will always remember him.

 We also went to Ottawa that same year to play in the National Jazz Competition. Across from our rooms at the hotel was this group of girls who were in a jazz choir from Vancouver. There was this cute blonde that flirted with me every time she saw me, so I decided to try and get to know her better. She invited me to her room one night and we fooled around. No biggie. However the next night she ended up hooking up with the rest of the rhythm section. When her friend went to get her to come out of their room, she freaked. I guess she was trying to protect her squeaky clean reputation (yeah right). She flipped out and called the cops and claimed these guys forcibly confined her, sexually assaulted her and whatnot. The cops carted Brad, Ben and Sean off to the clinker. I was like "No way these guys did that". They were wild like me but not stupid. She was full on charging these guys. So of course guess who got subpoenaed to testify as their character witness. Not only that, I had to go on the stand and talk about how I fingered this chick! I remember their lawyer had me on the stand and was like *"So what was her reaction as you were petting her vagina? and was there penetration?"* I friggin turned red as I had to blurt out in front of a packed courtroom, "Uhhhmmm, she seemed to be enjoying it?" Their lawyer made a mess of this girl and she ended up dropping the charges. Those fuckers still owe me a drink for saving their asses!

    I enrolled in college in the fall for marketing. Why, I still don't know. I looked so outta place there it wasn't funny. Here's this guy in skin tight jeans with snakeskin boots and huge hair trolling around this campus. Come the next year I was never there and just faded from that place. My parents were slowly giving up on me at this point and just shrugged their shoulders.

    1988 was great, there was so much killer rock coming out, I just ensconced myself in it. I was vicariously living through these bands. I figured, if I partied and acted like a rock star, I would of course become one.

Brian Majcenic: Fellow Toronto musician and long time friend

There was a time when a friend of ours threw a bunch of house parties when his parents were out of town on a long vacation. I remember the night when Stacey was browsing behind the bar and he discovered for the first time a bottle of (Seagram's?) Lemon Gin. It didn't take more than a few drinks for a healthy relationship to develop between the two. Whenever we ended up back at this house, he would walk in and say, with enthusiasm, "Crack open that lemon gin!" Now, the bar in this house was located down a long flight of stairs into a basement that was finished, from the top of the stairs down, with thick, bright, wall-to-wall orange shag carpeting. One night, with a full house, Stace cracked open the lemon gin enough times that at one point he missed the first stair when he was on his way down to the bar. I happened to be sitting on a couch by the bar. When I looked up, I watched him rapidly bouncing down every stair on his ass and then somehow, all in one continuous motion land perfectly upright on the ground. He walked straight to the bar without missing a beat. I still have the scars from laughing, but I'm convinced that carpet literally saved his ass that night. "Crack open that lemon gin!"

That year I discovered L.A. Guns. I remember buying the first record and when I flipped the back of the album over, the black and white photo they had spoke volumes to me. Not since I'd opened up *"Shout at the Devil"* by Motley Crue had a band picture moved me like that first L.A. Guns album. It was everything I wanted to be. It still trips me out that I became a permanent member in that band. Blind Desire was still gigging throughout '88 but I could feel it slipping away.

Forward to 1989. So here I go again. Dean and I started

another band called Heaven Sennt. We fuckin sucked and I started to really lose my focus. I was more concerned about our look than how my band sounded.

At this point in my life, I felt I needed to be free. I was 20 and had been going out with Cheryl now for over four years. I dumped her like an idiot and crushed her. Stupid me, a month later I was like "I fucked up please take me back." She flat out told me NO! Then proceeded to torture me for the next two years! She was the one who ended up crushing me. I think that's called "poetic justice." She actually took me back for a weekend and then vanished for three days. When I finally got a hold of her she wigged out on me and told me that she didn't want me back after all. To make matters worse she started going out with someone else right away. It fuckin killed me to think of someone else being with her. Cheryl would love to call me and knock me down and say shit like, "Well he loves me and I love him!" Can you hang on a minute while I take the knife you just plunged in my heart out? I guess I deserved it. I mean I was the one who dumped her and broke her heart.

My life was starting to crumble. I was convinced my mom was going crazy. She berated me on a daily basis. She just couldn't accept me for who I was. My dad would chime in every now and then, but I heard it from my mother on a daily basis. On top of that my sister had become estranged from my parents, which certainly didn't help things at home. Not to mention I dropped out of college. Big surprise right?

My parents were really starting to grind on me about my hair and the way I dressed. My dad was a fitness guru and would jog about six or seven miles a day. One Saturday he came in from his jog and sat on the couch. I noticed his hair was all fucked up and he looked like he had tried to spike it with my hair gel. I said "what's the deal with your hair, it looks ridiculous. His response was, "well now you know what you look like."

Around this time I became good friends with this singer Brian who played in another local metal band. Brian was a great guy and really was one of the only other guys in my neighborhood that dressed like me. Brian was into all the same cool bands, like L.A. Guns, Faster Pussycat, Kix, etc.

Towards the end of '89 I decided to get the hell out of town and go to L.A. for a week. I wanted to experience everything I had read and saw about the Sunset Strip. Me and my friend Ed who sang in Heaven Sennt, booked our tickets and hotel. Fuckin Hollywood here we come! So we are at the airport and so stoked to be going and Ed says to me "hey dude I got some pot on me." "Dude are you crazy! Ditch that shit!" I think he actually ate what he had on him. So we go through Customs and the Customs officer says to Ed "have you ever been arrested?" and he stupidly says yes! I almost kicked him in the foot just before that idiot blurted out yes. So, they haul him off to this room. Little did I know that Ed had been arrested for drugs three years earlier. All they did was punch his name into a computer and that's all she wrote. "Sorry sir but we can't let you into the States." My fuckin eyes bugged out, then realized I was going to L.A. by myself. Thanks for ruining my trip dude! I'm freaking the whole way there on the plane. What the fuck am I going to do in L.A. for eight days alone? I didn't know a soul there!

I called my buddy Brian who was thinking of coming with us from the airplane. When I called him he was like, "where the hell are you calling me from?" "I'm on the plane bro, Ed didn't make it through customs, you got to come and meet me out here!" Brian never made it to L.A.

Brian Majcenic:

We used to call each other from some random places. Nothing too crazy, but you never knew what to expect when picking up the phone. I had convinced Stacey to check out the music scene in L.A. for a week or two and he and a mutual friend decided to pack up and do it. During the morning of their flight, I got a call at home. It was Stace. "Hey, man!" he said.
"Dude! Where are you?" I asked.
"I'm on the plane!"
I was almost afraid to ask. "You're on the plane?"
"Yeah. Listen, there was a problem at the border. Can you get down to L.A., like, now?" As it turns out, the said mutual friend was denied a border crossing for more than one reason, so Stace was going solo. Unfortunately, I couldn't make it down, but I think it was the beginning of a full circle for Stacey. The next random call I got from him was from Florida when he was playing in Roxx Gang. The last one was when he crossed the country and hooked up with L.A. Guns.

Funny thing is I ran into this guitar teacher I knew from Toronto who happened to be living there. Same side of Melrose, same time of day, you get the idea. He was shocked to see me and took me out for many, many cold ones. I had a blast that day and hung out with Rob a few more times. I came back from my trip wanting to move there sooo bad. The Strip was at its peak and it was fuckin amazing. It was great hanging at the Rainbow, the Cathouse, Gazzari's and the Roxy. Of course I was by myself most of the time which completely sucked. I felt like I was living there. I soaked up the sun, shopped and went sight seeing.

Back to Toronto, which meant back to nothing. I thought my parents had written me off. I was still crushed inside from Cheryl and I was bandless. After I got back from L.A., I had the bright idea of joining this cover band that toured around the circuit in Ontario. I figured it was a good way to get me out of the house, away from my parents and make money at the same time. It was one of the most miserable experiences of my life! It was the middle of winter for starters and I hated going up on stage every night playing cover songs. The gigs were hit or miss. We would usually do a three day stint at a venue and then pack everything up and be onto the next town. The accommodations the venues supplied were horrendous. About the second week into the tour we were playing this shithole in Northern Ontario called Cochran. It was a small town about ten hours north of Toronto. The second night there were these three Native American girls and one of them had her scopes on me the whole night. She wouldn't leave me alone and then followed me up to my room. She refused to leave and finally I had to grab her by the hair and throw her ass out. The next day her and her two friends cornered me on the street and laid some kind of Shaman curse on me. I usually don't believe in that kind of stuff but things really started to get bad and these chicks weren't fooling around. An hour later the cops showed up and said "Well boys, I've got some bad news. Your soundman was injured in a car accident and your cube van is demolished." Basically what that meant is that we were fucked! We had no way now of leaving and getting to the next gig. All this weird shit started to happen. I lost a $100 bucks, I had this rash all over my body, my ghetto blaster took a shit, I woke up the next morning with a knot in my hair the size of a softball, some drunk chick threw a glass ashtray at my head and this whole shithole town had daggers for me. We ended up doing another two weeks in this hell hole till we could get the van fixed. Our singer decided to quit and I recruited my buddy Brian. He took the train all the way up to Cochran and even after a couple of weeks he said "Fuck this, this blows." He was right. A month later I had decided that this was enough and quit.

A few months later in Toronto, I met this cool singer named Mick. He had lots of tattoos and spiky blonde hair. We wanted to start a band like Faster Pussycat and L.A. Guns (little did I know I would end up in that band 13 years later). I knew three other guys with black hair that weren't in a band at the time and Fraidy Katt was born! I thought to myself, "God I hope this is the one." Story of my life is plain and simple ...

DOLLAR SHORT AND A DAY LATE

Fraidy Katt was a fantastic band. We looked fuckin cool and had all these radio catchy sleazy songs. Not only that but we had a ballad called "*No Shoulder to Cry On*" that was a sure fire hit. We spent so much time rehearsing, writing and demoing that by the time we were ready to blast our canons, hard rock and metal were starting to dye.

Fuck I'm never going to fuckin make it!!!

*Bruce Clark: Ex-Fraidy Katt Guitarist and long
             Long time friend*

What can I say about Stacey, well… We met in a local music store where we both frequented back in '86. I was there one day playing a couple of guitars, when he walked in and started talking to the owner about finding a bass player for his band. After talking and hearing what they played, I offered to come check them out at their rehearsal spot. History was made.
Stacey and I played together off and on for the next 5 years in different bands.
I remember writing songs over the phone with guitar in hand! Stacey always had good riffs, and pulled together arrangements that still impress me today, and in record time. Whole songs with the works. I learned a lot of guitar playing from him.
I still listen to him to this day and I have most, well… all of his commercial stuff, (and a few tapes from back in the early years).
Stacey was always driven like a muthafuka! When we were teenagers, his room (and all his residences) had two things; furniture…and his gear. No Frills!
One weekend sticks out in my mind, yeah there were many. We had a couple of shows booked that weekend, in the two leading rock bars in town. Thursday night at Rock n' Roll Heaven, (had the best layout and vibe ever), and Friday and Saturday at the loudest place on earth at the time, The Gasworks.
Well, Thursday night our bass player Rob at the time, (this is back in Fraidy Katt. Damn that was a good band!) Anyways, the night of our show, BAM! Serious snow storm, we're talking four feet, no

shit! Rob ends up being late 'cause he lived out of town at the time. Ten minutes before the show, he calls and tells us he's snowed in! There's me and Stacey, going over his bass lines with me on his bass, an original, full size, BC Rich Warlock, and Stacey ripping through the guitar tracks making it a 4 piece show…in ten minutes! And yes, we pulled it off!

The next night, we were opening for a local fave Jack Damage. At that time they RULED the Gasworks. The owner LOVED them. And they packed the place every time. During one of his solos, Stacey jumped out onto one of the monitor stands that was facing the stage. Little did he know that the stand was in fact a single post table that wobbled and flipped when he hit it. Wipe out! I'll never forget seeing Stacey attempt to climb back on stage with tight leather pants on! He made it though, and it was such a goodshow we had a laugh about it backstage. Later in the set, on a ballad, I broke a string on the last chord of the song. No problem, grab my spare, plug it in, strum and …WAAAAAAHHHH! Outta tune! Well the cold fucked up the tuning on the guitars, so when we checked them earlier we had to wait for them to warm up then tune. They didn't have enough time to warm up, we were pressed for time, so they went out of tune again when they warmed fully.

Our singer Mick turns and says, "Tune that fuckin thing…wait.. fuck it we're gonna play it anyway, 1,2,3,4…. and went into our next track. So we played, me out of tune, bending the neck, single notes, and muting the strings and Stacey, trying to figure out what I was playing. Rounds of applause and kudos from Jack Damage, just for having the balls, and saying fuck it, "Sink or Swim"

Even with all the fuck ups, that is one of my favorite weekends. I remember thinking "it doesn't get better than this!" If I died and could re-live those three days over and over for eternity, I would be a happy man. (Although I would change the pants I wore!)

Stacey and I worked well together. He's always been a live guy and always pulls the wickedest hook out of his ass when you least expect it.

 O.K. here is a short list of "Stacey'isms" (some of these are between me and him);

- Falling off stage with tight leather pants on.
- Stepping on his chord and unplugging during his solo. (I have it on video tape)
- Likes his guitar sound in "STEREO."
- Likes Cheese snacks, Tuna sandwiches, 2 liter bottles of Barbarian

Cooler, and six packs of Corona.

I honestly think when I look back at us at that time, I know for a fact he loved and still loves 1 thing, playing rock guitar. "Sink or Swim."

Fraidy Katt Feature—M.E.A.T. Magazine '91

L to R: Bruce, Stacey, Grant, Mick and Robbie

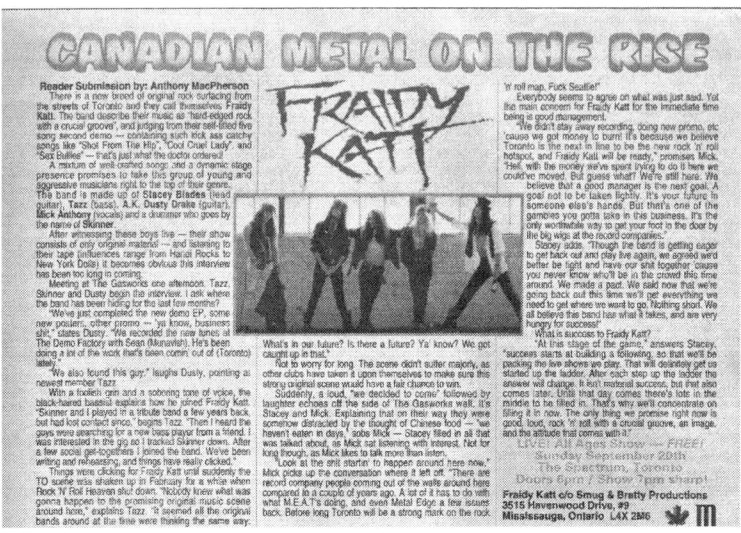

My mother and I at this point were really not getting along at all. I was working at Labatt's Brewery at the time. God I hated that job but the money was insane. I think my mom realized "Why am I not charging this kid rent?" I got in this huge fight with her. We had this really nice console table in the front foyer of our house. As I was screaming at my mom I decided to throw my wallet at her. In Canada we had these dollar coins called Looney's. They were pretty big and thick. I had about seven or eight of them in my wallet. I threw my wallet with such force that the Looney coins came flying out and shredded the finish of this table like a round out of an AK-47. Smart move asshole! I had to pay to get that stupid table refinished and it cost me almost 400 bucks!

My mom had finally decided I was outta here! She gave me a date in the last week of May that I was to be gone and I mean gone! When my mother kicked me out, I don't think my dad wanted me to go. I remember him yelling at mother: "You're not teaching him anything by kicking him out!" But it was for the best. I remember my mom saying to me "Have you found a place yet?" No I haven't, "No problem, because I found a place for you!" She wanted me gone so bad that she actually got an apartment for me! I was more than ready to be on my own, trust me.

Shirley Ingram:
Stacey and I had our disagreements and fights over the years with a few threats of "if you do that again.........." thrown in for effect. We were really at each others throats a lot of the time. After one of these famous fights we used to have, he came out of his room and whatever he had in his hand he let fly. It hit a new table in our front hall and as it skimmed across and onto the floor I decided it was time for another lesson in life. $350 later I think he may have learned to think before acting.

Around late '90 I started to go out with this black haired beauty named Gypsy who was a complete fuckin lunatic! I met her one night at this rock club called the Opera House. We made eye contact at the bar and I was blown away at how hot she was. She said I looked like Phil Lewis as a matter of fact. We started dating shortly after that and she moved in with me. Something I wish I had thought through. Unfortunately, I'd follow this pattern for years to come.

Gypsy in our apartment-
'91 and her cat that hated me.

STARS IN HIS EYES

CHAPTER 3

Gypsy and I moved into this basement apartment below this old Italian couple. It fuckin sucked. They were always down there getting something out of their cellar. Gypsy put me through hell as well. She would get all fucked up and then go Jekyll and Hyde on my ass. There was one night where Gypsy came home from a party all fucked up and started to get weird with me which of course led to a fight. This resulted in me getting kicked in the face by her. The landlord, Giuseppe came downstairs and wondered what the hell was going on. Gypsy very subtlety turned around and said "Fuck you Giuseppe." The look on that guy's face was priceless.

I was crumbling on the inside. I was convinced my mom hated me, and I had this complete lunatic girlfriend. We then moved into another hell hole. Why I kept choosing the basement of a house to rent, I'm not sure. Above us was this young Pakistani couple. The guy was so nice and they had a kid who would proceed to tell me to get out of his yard every time he saw me. I wanted to wring that little fucker's neck. This guy's chick was a complete psycho. She used to scream at him (insert Pakistani accent) *"Do you vant to die! I vill kill you!!!"* I think she even stabbed the poor guy a few times.

The house next to us had this deep sunken driveway that leveled off from my front walkway. One drunken night Gypsy and I took a cab home from this party where she proceeded to punch me in the face. I had to run in to get some cash for the cab and Gypsy was starting to turn on me once again. As I was running back out, I tripped over the curb and dropped 6 feet onto the driveway next door. Nice move! I tore the shit out of my knee and it was another great moment in our relationship. I limped back to the apartment all bloody and torn and there's Gypsy starting to demolish the place once again.

    I would spend every weekend at Rock N Roll Heaven (still one of the best rock bars I have ever seen) decked out in full L.A. rock star regalia……….. Black leather gloves, leather jacket, polka dot shirt, crushed velvet tights and black steel tipped cowboy boots and big black spiky hair. RNR Heaven was the closest thing to being in L.A. you could get. It was the place to go, play, see and be seen. Every chick was decked out and every cool rocker was there hangin' and drinking. I would just hang in the back horseshoe bar there and get fucked up and look cool as possible, that's if I wasn't fighting with Gypsy. I remember the first time Fraidy Katt headlined there, it was in the winter and there was this huge snowstorm. Imagine how that night turned out. I really believed that there were other forces at work to prevent me from being a rock star. I would fall into bouts of depression

Fraidy Katt Headlining RnR Heaven during a snowstorm—'91

and numb myself with tons of alcohol. However, the more I did this Gypsy would do the same and end up tearing our place up. She was a complete nut but so pretty I would just put up with it.

We ended up moving into this building uptown. Her mom lived 2 floors above us and there were always these strange little secrets they would

Promo Shot—'91

hide. Fuck at times I was convinced they were in protective custody by the FBI. If I was to ever ask her about her dad she would go mental. I never did find out the truth about those two. I remember my buddy Bruce had told me years later that he had seen Gypsy strung out on the streets in Toronto and it broke my heart to hear that.

During the summer of '90 Robbie, Fraidy Katt's bassist got married. The whole band were the ushers and it was a kick ass wedding. The reception was held outside and of course it poured cats and dogs that day. They had erected this huge tent in his wife's parent's backyard. All these poor people were getting soaked while they stood in line for their food.

Our drummer's sister was at the wedding. I can't remember her name but she was the female version of Chris Farley. She got completely rotted at the wedding. They had set up this mock type dance floor with a separate tent to cover it. Grant's sister was dancing like a maniac and we were all in stitches as she tore it up! She started going ballistic when the DJ played "Babylon" by Faster Pussycat. She started doing this zombie stomp and started swinging at people. She made a b-line for me and as she was about three feet away her feet completely came out from under her and she just hung in the air and then came crashing down hard. I think me and the rest of the band pissed ourselves with laughter. That fall really hit Grant's sister and she just sat there for a minute not knowing what to do.

Fraidy Katt had this smoking demo by mid '91. Of course L.A. style hard rock was pretty much coming to a halt by then. We were gigging and starting to make some noise and then Robbie the bassist quits. He was our bro and we were devastated. Fuck here we go again, I just can't win dammit! We got this other guy but it wasn't the same without Robbie. Then three months later Mick says he's quitting and moving to L.A. Well that's fuckin it! It felt like all my hard work and dreams just got flushed down the toilet along with my sanity! I was one of most driven dudes and I just couldn't catch a break!

I started working at this Custom Broker downtown. I was a runner, which means I would take documents to and from the office to shipping companies and collect documents from Customs as well. It was a cake job. I would cruise around downtown with my briefcase most of the day and the money was good. I was bandless at the time and was starting to get disillusioned with my so-called music career. Not only that but Gypsy and I had broken up and were still living together. I was losin' it really quickly.

One afternoon at work Cheryl called my office and asked if I wanted to go to lunch. I was completely shocked. I hadn't talked to her in months. I was so nervous to see her. So she meets me a couple blocks from my office. The moment I saw her, my heart sank! I still really loved her as much as she broke my heart. We spent that hour together and all she did was fuckin babble about furniture her and her boyfriend had bought. I think she was trying to make me jealous or something. She kept staring at me. I must admit I looked really good that day, I remember, hahaha. She left after the hour or so and as she was walking away she just had this longing in her eyes for me, but I just kept my mouth shut. If I had opened it, who knows how the rest of my life would've turned out. That was the last time I ever saw her. Years later I would still wonder whatever became of her, I bet she does the same with me or maybe she doesn't. She must have memory burned me because I still to this day have vivid dreams of her.

I started dating this tiny cute little blonde named Tracy. After three dates I asked her if she wanted to go to the Caribbean with me. I was on the verge of a nervous breakdown. I had to get away from Gypsy, my apartment, my job and my life. We went to some shabby resort on the south side of Cuba. It was right on the Caribbean and all the food and booze were included. Tracy and I soaked up the sun, ate, drank and shagged. However, one night I took it a little too far (like I did with everything). We started partying with a bunch of people around 7 pm. I started drinking Cuban rum and coke. Come midnight I had polished off about 20 off them. I was fuckin hammered and we took the party down to the beach bar. I started to get out of control and almost beat up some old French fuck. Tracy was getting fed up with my drunken ass and split back to the room. That should have been my cue to split, but like true Stacey Blades fashion, I can't stop the party! Next thing I know I passed out standing up. I did a face plant right into the marble floor! Fucked up my face and chipped my tooth; nicely done. A few guys carried me across the beach and just left me by the pool.

Sun Bathing in Cuba--1992

Some guy saw me staggering around the pool and gracefully carried me back to my room. I really believed this guy saved my life that night. There was a good chance I would have fallen in that pool and drowned. I got to the room and Tracy was pissed! I passed out and woke up the next day and was still drunk. I staggered down to the beach and went to the bar to nurse my hangover. This guy goes to me "how's your face feeling?" I said "huh?" He goes "you don't remember me do you." I'm like no I don't. "I carried you back to your room." I felt like the biggest tool in the world at that point. I thanked him and said can I make it up to you? He said don't sweat it. We were leaving the next day. Thank God 'cause I felt like I had alcohol poisoning.

So, back to reality, my job, Gypsy and my apartment. Things were really awkward at home for the next few months. Fortunately we had a two bedroom apartment so I took the second bedroom, though it really didn't help matters. While I was doing my usual route for the Custom Broker, I stopped at a magazine stand like I usually would do and starting thumbing through the new copy of Metal Edge. I noticed an ad that said Roxx Gang was looking for a guitarist. I freaked. I had their album and really liked that band. Their look and sound was right up my alley. I thought I totally could get this gig and they were a national band and from the States. This was my ticket outta here! I just said "I'm getting this gig and that's all there is to it." I called their manager when I got home and they told me to send them a press package. I got on it right away. I did a killer photo shoot, made a copy of the Fraidy Katt Demo and Fed-Ex'd that thing pronto. Days after they got it they called me and said the band really digs you and your playing. Ah yes! There was a light at the end of the tunnel. They said book a flight down here (St. Petersburg, Fla.) and we'll set up an audition, which of course I did immediately. I booked some time off from work. Around that time there was this wicked flu going around my office. I was like, "I'll be damned if I catch this thing". Sure enough the night before I left, I started to get sick. This wasn't just any flu this was like the king of all flu's. I got to the airport and my flight had been delayed like five hours. I was like you've got to be kidding me! I started to lose my voice and was feeling really sick. Here we fuckin go again! I felt that force trying to hold me back again. Not this time, no way! I finally got into Tampa seven hours later than I was supposed to. The manager and his girlfriend picked me up and took me out for a drink. Even as sick as I was I still managed to knock back 4 Jack and Cokes.

I stayed at some shithole Super 8 Hotel or something. I woke up the next morning at like 7 and started practicing. They had told me to learn four or five songs off the first record. I think it was "*Scratch My Back, Fastest Gun in Town, Red Rose and Ball and Chain*." Fuck if I didn't know those songs inside and out. 1'oclock rolled around and the manager picked me up in his piece of rusted out shit car. I thought, fuck did these guys sell any records or pay this guy to manage them? Their manager was the singer's brother. We rolled over to the rehearsal studio in this car with no A.C. I made sure I looked stellar. I had this black vest on and tight black pants with pointy purple suede boots. My hair was perfect! However I felt like I was dying from this flu. I walked into the waiting area and there's all these rockers with their guitars waiting. It felt a little awkward. So, here comes my turn. I walked in like I owned the place. I said hello to everybody, then plugged my B.C. Rich Gunslinger into the Marshall amp fired it up as I felt my knees buckle but was ready to kick ass. We played five or six songs and it felt like we had good chemistry. I could tell while I was playing, the guys were digging me and I was digging rockin with the Gang. After we were done they brought this other kid in from Texas. He was a nice guy and thought he had a great look. This poor guy had taken the bloody bus all the way from Dallas for the audition. I guess they figured since I did so well, let's see how I and the rest of the band play with this other kid. It sounded pretty good but I think I was a little more prepared than the kid from Texas. Nevertheless, I liked him. I was hoping they would add him as well since Roxx Gang was a two guitar player band. Needless to say they never pursued him.

After we were done, the bassist Roby Strine went over to the bar beside the studio and told the manager to grab this guy right now! (That felt really good to hear later). All the guys were really happy with the audition. I was stoked! I knew I nailed it. Brett dropped me back off at the Super 8 and told me I had been the best they had all week. I knew I was getting this gig!

I settled back into my room and crashed! So I went back to Toronto the next morning. I felt like hell and that flu knocked me out for four days. Later that week Brett phoned and told me I got the gig! I was jumping for joy and finally felt like I was on my way to doing something great. Brett told me to get ready! He was sending me 20 more songs to learn and said that they had a deal with Atlantic pretty much wrapped up. Brett was good at blowing smoke up people's asses! I would soon find this out the hard way.

I was so excited and called my parents to tell them I got the gig and was moving to Florida. They kind of hesitated and said are you sure this is something you want to do? I couldn't believe it! No "Congratulations that's great!" I still fuckin couldn't get their damn approval. It really crushed me. I just scored the gig of my life and they were like "okay?"

SOUTH OF THE BORDER

CHAPTER 4

That Monday morning I gave my notice at work. I couldn't wait to tell my boss, who was a prick, that I was outta here and moving to the States to do music full-time. I told Brett, Roxx Gang's manager that I needed three weeks to get ready for the move. That would give me the time to learn those 20 songs. I had my work cut out for me, but I was stoked and excited. I knew my life wasn't going to be the same in three weeks. I booked another flight and tried to sell everything I didn't need. I only went with my suitcase and my guitars. My mom shipped some stuff to me three months later.

When I broke the news to Gypsy she seemed sad. It shocked me a little, because I thought this chick hated me. Maybe she really did care. She could've fooled me every time she threw something at me like a bowl of spaghetti. My rocker buddies took me out for a congratulatory night of cold beers.

After a couple of weeks of living, eating and breathing Roxx Gang, I was chilling out on the couch when it felt like I was having a heart attack! I jolted up off the couch in a complete panic. Little did I know I was having a major anxiety attack. It had all crept up on me. I was leaving everything behind. All my friends, my family, and my twisted ex-girlfriend. I was the first guy to sacrifice everything if it meant me furthering my music career. So here comes leaving day! I had $1500, my guitar and my luggage. Gypsy had to work that morning and my mom was picking me up so I could stay at their house to get a ride to the airport. I must have had an early flight. When Gypsy was getting ready to leave, she just started to burst into tears, which made me start to cry as well. I think we both realized that as fucked up as our relationship was we were probably never going to see each other again. It took this to have our feelings come full circle I guess. She called me 20 minutes after she left and broke down again saying she didn't know what she was going to do without me. This was a really tough day. I knew I wasn't going to see my family for a long time as well.

So I'm going through customs at the airport and they pull me into this room. Back then those guys usually really had it in for the rockers. The guy was fuckin grilling me and went through my wallet. The customs guy actually told me they were going to be monitoring my movements in Florida. I was like "Have I done something wrong?" I guess he realized he was being a prick and said "Have a nice trip". The flight was bumpy as hell and my nerves were friggin rattled! Kevin Steele (singer in R.G) picked me up at the tiny little St. Petersburg airport. I said do you mind if we stop so I can get a six pack. It had been a hell of a 24 hour period. Kevin and I really hit it off. He let me stay with him for a couple of weeks till I got settled. However our relationship would soon deteriorate after his constant brow beating and I would grow to hate that guy.

Now as excited as I was, I never really wanted to be that "replacement guy". It was always my dream to start something from the ground up and make that dream come alive! Being that replacement guy always comes with questions and such a long story of explanation "Well you see I got the gig because the original guy was all fucked up on drugs and the band really wanted to sack him blah blah blah………. We started rehearsing and writing right away. I just couldn't understand why these guys waited 6 long months to book a show. I was ready now!

One night Roby took me to the local big rock club M.L. Chasers. We were completely decked out in black vinyl pants and tight vests. I remember when I walked in I realized I was not in Kansas anymore. Everyone in that fuckin place looked at me at once. It was weird, I was a dime a dozen in Toronto but here in South Florida the only other guys that looked like me were in the band! Word spread pretty quick about me being the new guy in town and the chicks started to get real friendly quick. One night I picked up this girl and she asked if I wanted to go for a ride. I didn't know my way around and forgot where Kevin lived. The chick was either stupid or pretended to be lost as we started to drive out to the beach. Next thing I know the cops pull her over. She was very close to getting a DUI, I told the cops I was in Roxx Gang and they actually let her go! Being in a name band does have its perks.

After a few weeks I moved in with this bartender named Mike. The place was a nightmare and his teenage daughter was always having her friends over and that got old really quick. I met this stripper named Pam through a friend of Mike's. She seemed like a cool girl, Wrong! I soon found out I had another psycho on my hands. I came home one day and Mike had conveniently forgotten to pay the power and water bill and left a turd floating in the toilet. That was it, I had been paying money for the bills and I guess he wasn't paying them. Not only that but him and his daughter were eating all my food! I called Pam and she came over and said grab your stuff you're moving in with me! No problem, she lived in a killer apartment complex and I thought things would only get better, NOT! After a month or so she started acting really weird. She would come home really, really late at night and then act all aloof. She came home one day and said pack up your stuff you're outta here and my ex-boyfriend is coming over. I was floored. I was like "Is this really happening?" I grabbed my stuff and all my clothes and sat out in the parking lot while my friend Sue came and picked me up. Pam walked right past me with her ex and didn't even bat an eye. All I could think was "What a fuckin bitch!" What the hell did I do to her!

Welcome to PLANET FLORIDA FUCKER!

I soon found out that this state was full of douche bags and weirdos. (Maybe it was just the company I kept). So Sue let me stay with her for a while. She was an angel with the biggest heart I've ever seen. I thought I was joining this band that had been on MTV and been in every metal magazine and here I was living like a pauper. I started to really freak out. Not only that but after the first show I remember asking Brett for my show pay and he flipped out on me! Just where was that $1500 all going to? That should have been my first clue right there.

I decided I needed to go home for a week. I needed to see my real friends and see my mom and dad. I booked a flight to Toronto for a week. I remember Brett and Kevin were convinced that I wasn't coming back. My first six months were off to a rough start.

So I went home and Gypsy met me at my parents. I was so excited to see her. I just melted in her arms. The first few nights I caught up with friends and went out and had a blast. It felt good to be home. However by the middle of the week Gypsy started to act like a total weirdo and I had this feeling like I wasn't supposed to be here anymore. What's that they say when you move away "You can never go home?" That saying was ringing in my head like a jackhammer. I said bye to Gypsy and she seemed like she could've cared less. I never saw her again.

When I got back to Florida things started to get better. We had another big show and we were heading into the studio to lay down a ton of new tracks. We started working with Ric Browde. He produced Poison, Faster Pussycat and Joan Jett to boot. Ric tried to get us a deal but really at the end of the day didn't have all that much input. We also shot a video for the song "Time Bomb." We figured it was a good tool to use while we were shopping a new deal. It was my first video shoot and let me tell you it was hard work. Eight hours doing the same performance shots. We shot in black and white and set up the shoot at this Pepsi warehouse. Christian Moriarty who worked for Playboy and also shot videos for 2 Live Crew shot it and went on to film another three videos with us.

A few weeks later, we're playing to a packed house at M.L. Chasers and who do I see out in the audience but Pam. Then she comes up right to the front of the stage and is just staring at me. She placed a dagger earring I left at her place on my Wah Pedal. We would always end the show with "*Red Rose.*" Pam comes back up to the very front of the stage and then proceeds to start crying. I could hear the psycho sirens going off in my head. WTF!

After a local show we would always go back to Kevin's house for a raging party. So I'm sitting down at the table having drinks with Roby and I feel this tap on my shoulder. I turn around and it's Pam! She had just walked into Kevin's without knocking or nothing. I was like "what the hell are you doing here!" Kevin's girlfriend started yelling at her to get the fuck out! So I walked outside to talk to her, why I don't know. She lays this shit on me that she's pregnant with my kid! I was like "No Fucking Way!" I know when I'm being played. She had probably realized that she shouldn't have dumped me and was trying to lure me back into her twisted life. What am I? A psycho magnet or what!

IT'S A JUNGLE OUT THERE

<u>Chapter 5</u>

Pam was just the beginning of many sorted women I would date over the next six years. After the Pam debacle I started dating this dingbat named Jenny. She was obsessed with manatees. She would always say in her dingbat high voice "Look Stacey manatees." Jenny had a twin sister named Julie. I had met her through this guy Kenny who owned a big rock n'roll clothing store named Wild Child. He also ran a baseball team which I joined that had all the local rockers on it. We totally sucked and would get our asses handed to us every game we played. It was a lot of fun because after we lost, we would always go to a bar and down tons of pitchers of beer.

So when I started to date Jenny she was also dating this singer in another band. We both didn't know and she played us very well. I remember one night hanging out at M.L. Chasers and I was convinced I saw Jenny with this guy. I said to her friends "Did I just see Jenny with that guy Jeff?" Her friends immediately started to distract me with band questions as one of them ran to Jenny to tip her off. I later found out that at Christmas she was running shifts between me and this other dude. First she invited me over to her mother's place and then brought me home because she had to go to her aunt's. Then she would have Jeff come over to her mother's for the afternoon shift. Real winner huh!

Around this time I met this young girl Selene who was an absolute angel and would become one of my very best friends to this day. By the way, she was the one who distracted me at the bar, hahaha. Selene was dating this goofy guy who also had a twin brother. She was miserable and I would lecture her, usually in a drunken stupor to ditch this loser and share my so- called wisdom with her. I imagine the voice inside her head was like "Who does this dude think he is with his giant black long hair, leather pants and purple suede boots telling me how to live my life."

Getting back to the softball team, I became friends with this girl Mina. She was from Finland but lived in New York City for quite a few years. She was a total cutie but so hard to understand. Her accent was completely half Finnish and half New York. I took Mina out a few times but nothing really ever came of it. Plus she had a baby so it was almost impossible for her to go out. Ironically this girl was Kelly Nickels (original L.A. Guns bassist) first wife! Six degrees of L.A. Guns right!

The next year was like a revolving door of dumb bitches. I remember this girl Holly saying to me "Gee Stacey you sure like to date a lot of women". "That's because I can!" I replied back. But what I really wanted to say was that I just can't find a nice girl. (My mom kept telling me to go to a church and find a nice girl, she couldn't have been more right).

So I finally settled into a decent living situation. My friend Sue's friend Mike needed a roommate and he was a great guy and a guitar player as well. His cousin was married to Keith Richards. Living with Mike was perfect because he was never there. I must have had a different girl in that place every week. The few times Mike was there he just had this look like "Dude you're the man!" Mike spent practically all his time over at his girlfriend's but really enjoyed his company when he was there. There were a lot of great nights hanging with Mike playing guitar, laughing and drinking beer and listening to music. He was the easiest going, laid back, funny guy I ever met. However, the poor guy must have had deep hidden depression because a year later he ended up hanging himself in his girlfriend's garage. This news devastated me and I had just talked to Mike two days earlier prior to him doing this. I felt like I had lost a real friend.

Roxx Gang was starting to gig a lot out of town. I remember this one show we did in Sarasota, Florida. The place was packed and the fans were acting like we were the friggin Beatles. It was amazing! We could barely get out of there, they were practically mobbing us. It was the first experience of that kind of adoration and I lapped every ounce of it up. I was really starting to have a good time in the band. Roby and I were tight. We would always get ourselves into trouble and we would egg each other on. We had gotten to the point of "Who could piss Brett and Kevin off more, you or me." Roby was like the little devil on my shoulder. I think he saw that raw, unbridled enthusiasm in my eyes. Roby would be like "Hey Dude c'mon lets kill a 6 pack each before we go on stage." Kevin was always like "I can't understand it; by the end of the shows the two of you are hammered." The fact of the matter was that we were! I can clearly remember just laughing up on stage because of being hammered and having so much fun. However there were certain times where it would show. There's no disguising playing a lead in a completely wrong key. I'm sure the booze had nothing to do with that. We totally had this care free swindle type Keith Richards attitude.

Roxx Gang Bassist Roby Strine and I partying after a show—'93

By mid '94 however I noticed Roby starting to act like he didn't give a shit anymore and looking back on it now I don't blame him. Sure enough after a rehearsal he told us he was quitting. I was really bummed. He was my only bud in the band. I started to have that sinking feeling again like I did so many times before when a band member would quit. Not only that but Roby was an original member as well. Kevin couldn't have been happier. That guy fuckin hated everybody! I don't think he ever said anything nice about anybody who was in the band before me. It made me start to think, "Were all those other original guys that bad or is it Kevin?"

So we replaced Roby with this cool tattooed, black haired cat named Dorian Sage. Dorian fit right in and played great as well. Dorian and I became blood brothers. Not only that, but he also DJ'd at Diamond Dolls which was a fantastic strip club. Fuck, I would spend every waking moment there when he worked. It gave me carte blanche at that place and I think I dated just about every stripper there. One afternoon I was hanging out there and I was waiting at the bar for my beer. I was wearing a black leather jacket and a black bolero hat. Some old dude says "Hey kid Halloween was over two weeks ago." That old prick was Evel Kinevel. I thought what an asshole! Not to mention the sheer idiocy of that statement considering the guy used to wear star spangled white satin jumpsuits! I think I flipped him off or something.

Dorian and I would go out a lot. We were hanging at this club in Tampa and ran into the bassist from this popular Florida band named Stranger. He came up to us and said "You guys want some blow?" I had never done cocaine and was totally against that shit. But of course Dorian and I went into the bathroom and jammed all that shit up our noses. I remember the owner of the club walked in at that exact moment and looked at us and said "What the hell are you guys doing! Go into the stall please!" We went back out to the bar and I felt like I was on top of a mountain with one of those trumpets with the tapestry on it. No wonder that shit was so addictive!

Around this time I decided to reach out to Kathy St. John, the girl I had my first crush on when I was a kid. I called her out of the blue and she was floored to hear from me. We talked over the next six to eight months. Kathy must have had demons inside her and fought fierce anxiety and depression. She had tried to off herself a few times with a hunting knife. I couldn't understand why she had all these dark feelings and depression. She was such a great kid. About a year later I got that dreaded call that Kathy had hanged herself and died. I was crushed. I had known this girl since I was seven and had rekindled my friendship with her over the last year. Not only that but it had been a year since my buddy Mike had also hanged himself.

Kathy St.John (R.I.P.) and I –Vancouver 1980

Anyways back to the dysfunction. One night at rehearsal Dorian was bragging about this porn star that was dancing at Diamond Dolls for the weekend and was staying at his condo. We were like "Oh who!" Lois Ayers! He replies. Lois Ayers was one of the biggest adult stars of the 80's. I guess Dorian used to hang out with her when he lived in L.A. back in the late 80's. Dorian said he was going to hang at the Double D (that's what we called Diamond Dolls) and asked if I would join him. So we go up there and it's Friday night. The place is rockin' and we're having a blast flirting with the girls and downing drinks. Dorian brings me backstage and introduces me to Lois. She was a fox and looked like she did in her movies. I was intrigued to meet her. I always wondered how these pretty girls would let themselves get wrapped up in such a racket like the porn industry. I guess they are usually fucked up to begin with. Anyways Lois seemed like such a sweetheart, it's too bad she did porn 'cause she seemed like such a nice girl. Anyways, later that night her chaperone comes up to me and says "Lois really likes you and wants to do a threesome with you and Dorian." Somehow this didn't come as a surprise. So after she's done dancing we take her back to my pad. By this time I'm hammered. Lois is sitting beside me on my sofa looking at me with lust in her eyes. Dorian whispers something in her ear and he walks off to my bedroom with her. I'm going "Hey what about me!" A few minutes later, Dorian then tells me to come into the bedroom. Lois is laying butt naked on my king size bed. Dorian looks at me and goes "Happy Birthday Bro!" and walks out of the bedroom. Like I said I was hammered and as I was hammering her I started to have double vision. I would look down and have two dicks. I later told this story to my buddies in Warrant who affectionately nicknamed me Stacey Twodixx. Of course you got to say it with an Andrew Dice Clay accent. Throughout the night I noticed Lois getting more and more fucked up. She was popping

Valium like they were Pez! Shit she could barely walk out of my pad at the end of night. I recently read the "Heroin Diaries", Nikki Sixx's new book which talked about an incident with Lois that made my skin crawl.

About 4 months prior I had taken a part-time job working for a timeshare company selling vacation packages over the phone. It was a pretty easy job, and I only worked five hours a day. The money was good but you would lose a lot of your commissions on cancellations. I had to work the next morning after the Lois affair. I went to bed a 5:30 am and had to be at work at 9:30 am. I was so fried I could barely walk. They ended up letting me go home (I had really cool boss's) because I couldn't form a word.

A few months later, I had moved in with my friend Tony and believe it or not Pam's ex-boyfriend Jeff. Jeff was alright and we did have one thing in common, we both agreed Pam was nuts! We were sharing an old three bedroom house. The house had been there since the 50's and we soon found out it was haunted. If you think I'm making this up, guess again. There were all kinds of weird shit that happened in that place. For starters, lights would go off and on all the time. There was a few times where I would flick a light switch and the light wouldn't go on, then I would turn around and the switch would be in the off position. That happened a lot. The weirdest was one day Jeff and I had gotten home at the same time one afternoon. Jeff was a hairstylist and had this make shift salon set up in the back of the house. All of the sudden we hear this tremendous crash! We walked back to that room and the big mirror Jeff had in there was laying split in half on the floor. What made this weird is that the mirror was leaning against the wall on a table with all kinds of hair care products in front of it. The table was completely undisturbed. In other words, it was as if someone had picked up the mirror from the table and smashed it on the floor. There is no chance in hell that mirror could have fallen without knocking down everything in front of it. Every time I took a shower, it felt like someone was watching me. I really got creeped out a few times. The worst was when I was alone one night watching television. I heard this coughing coming from the back of the house. I jolted up off the couch and muted the television and heard it again! I knew right then and there that there was something else in this house than just the three of us.

Tony knew this American Indian girl who practiced Shaman rituals. After a few hours in the house she said that we did indeed have a spirit and it was the original owner of the house. She also said that he died in the house of Tuberculoses. I said "What!" Well that explained the coughing I heard from the back of the house. She did this weird process of rubbing this oil on all the mirrors, and then burned candles in front of them. What was really strange is that after burning the candles the mirrors were ice cold. Strange shit let me tell you.

One of Tony's buddies brought this girl over with him one night. The whole time she was there, she just kept staring at me like I was a chicken dinner. She was tiny, blonde and cute as hell and reminded me of 80's video vixen Bobbi Brown, the girl from Warrant's "Cherry Pie" video. She came by the house again with this guy she was dating and about an hour after she left, she came back by herself and knocked on my bedroom door! She told me that she couldn't stop thinking of me and wanted to see more of me. No problem! I wish I would have told her no, because that little bitch put me through the wringer. She was so hot and innocent but had an attitude on her like a 40-year-old divorced Beverly Hills bitch.

Jamie and I- Roxx Gang Record Release Party '95

I should've known better than to get involved with her. She was a dancer and her cousin was a dancer and her aunt was a dancer and they all danced at that same damn bar! Sounds like a Jerry Springer episode. Jamie would taunt me, play me, and mess with my head. I would try to diss her so many times and she would come back and manipulate me with her big blue eyes and cute smile. I finally broke up with her, but she would still call me. Then she started dating my friend Matt who bartended at this bar I would hangout at. I just thought "Wow, there are a lot of backstabbing assholes in this town!"

    One night I decided to venture out to squash my frustrations about Jamie and went to one of the many strip joints I frequented. As I was knocking a few beers back I saw one of the dancers from Diamond Dolls that I somewhat knew. I can't remember her name but it was something stupid like Isis. She was a cool chick with bleach blonde hair and a little junk in the trunk but beautiful nonetheless. We hung out for a while and she asked if I wanted to head over the bay to Tampa and get a drink. I was like "sure, lead the way". We hoped in her killer new Porsche 911 and headed over to some stupid chic artsy disco. After a few hours of flirting and downing drinks, she grabbed my crotch and said let's go for a ride. As we drove back to Clearwater, she pulled the car over along side the causeway. Tampa and Clearwater/ St. Petersburg are connected by two Causeways over the water of Tampa Bay. The Courtney Campbell and the Howard Franklin. As we speed down the Courtney Campbell, she said "I have a wild idea" I said "oh yea, what do you have in mind?" "Have you ever done it in a Porsche?", "No I haven't." We parked the Porsche and started to make out. Isis then pulled me out of the car and pulled me on the hood. It was a perfectly balmy clear night and the full moon lit up my white ass as I banged Isis on the edge of Tampa Bay as cars whistled by honking at us. Thank you Isis for getting me out of my funk.

ILLUSIONS OF GRANDEUR

Chapter 6

By mid '95, Roxx Gang had finally landed somewhat of a deal. We signed with Perris Records and released "*The Voodoo You Love.*" We had a ton of tracks to choose from and ended up putting 12 songs on the CD. My parents had come down to Florida to visit me. We went to Spec's music and my mom ended up buying four copies of "*The Voodoo You Love.*" She said to the clerk when she was ringing them up "That's my son." I finally felt like I was getting their approval.

We launched the release of the CD with a record release party at none other than Diamond Dolls. It was a stellar night. The food and drink flowed and we had this killer stretch limo parked outside the whole night. Lots of press was there and a Florida based T.V. show Metal Masters came out to film the night. They made their rounds interviewing each member of the band. By the time they reached me I was half in the bag. What do you expect with an open bar! I remember they had to do three or four takes because I kept fucking up.

Roxx Gang Record Release Party '95

L to R: Kevin, Tommy, Stacey, Dorian

As Jamie and I were having problems I started getting chummy with her cousin Chris. Four months later I started dating her. This was not the best idea and I would live to regret that very move. But I'm a sucker for a pretty face.

When Jamie and I stopped seeing each other, I started dating this girl Kristina who I had met a few times out and about. I really wasn't into her that much but she was fun to hang out with. Hey, alcohol can make things more fun sometimes. After a few months I think we realized we didn't like each other that much and I think we told each other to f'off.

A few months later I was having a smoke break at work and my boss comes up to me and says, "Hey bro, I just got the strangest call? "Oh yeah" I replied. This girl had called about working here and after I gave her the address, she said "Oh shit, I can't work there, that's where Stacey from Roxx Gang works and my friend is having his kid!" I was like "WHAT!" I asked what her name was and I figured out it was Kristina's friend. One night when I was with Kristina, I noticed after we had sex the condom I was using broke. I did the math inside my head and it all made sense.

I called my friend Sue Erwin who was good friends with Kristina. "Sue, it's Stace, is Kristina pregnant with my kid?" There was this long pause, "Stacey how did you find out?" Ahhh shit! It was true. The weirdest part about it was that she was going to give the baby up for adoption. Sue also told me that Kristina was never even going to tell me!

This really was making my head spin. The whole adoption thing threw me into this really weird space. I couldn't handle knowing that there was going to be my flesh and blood out there somewhere not knowing who his real dad was, the same thing that plagued me for years.

I called Kristina and told her I knew and she said that it wasn't any of my concern and that her mind was already made up. I said, "Well I think it's some of my concern." Long story short, she ended up having a miscarriage. As bad as I felt for her, I was certainly relieved. I guess this child was just not meant to be born.

A few months after, Jamie's cousin Chris and I shacked up and ended up dating for a year and a half. Jamie found out six months into it and flipped! We really did a good job keeping this a secret from her. I remember one Christmas we went to her grandmother's. When Jamie walked in she gave me the worst dirty look I have ever seen in my life! Hey what can I say, paybacks are a bitch.

Around this time Dorian started to drift away from the band and we eventually let him go. There goes that revolving door again. Not only that but he started dating PAM! I couldn't believe it! I told him "Dude you don't know what you are doing getting involved with her, she's bad news bro!" He refused to listen to me and things weren't the same between us. So what did he do but marry that nut! He later would regret that very decision. It's funny over the next two years; two of my other band mates would start dating girls I went out with! It really pissed me off and I felt like I was trapped in a dark sitcom. Dorian told me later on that Pam had tried to run him over with his Camaro. That sounds like something she would've done. Years later when I was living in L.A., I was watching the Maury Povich show and they were doing something on teenagers who were bullied in high school or something. Low and behold Pam comes walking out. I about fell out of my seat.

Things with Christine got really bad.

Why the hell did I   a.) Go out with her and

b.) Move in with her

Christine treated me so bad! She would throw shit at me and mentally abuse me on a daily basis. There was one night I had decided to go out with Brett. When I came home later that night I found all my clothes thrown all over the living room. I was like "What the hell?" A few seconds later, Christine comes blasting out of the bedroom like Glenn Close in *"Fatal Attraction."* Chris had one of those thick white plastic hangers and proceeded to break that thing in half over my knuckles! I know I wasn't the easiest person to deal with, but shit this was complete psychotic behavior! Christine had really gotten the better of me and I got extremely depressed. Chris ended up kicking me out and started going out with this little weasel that DJ'd at the strip club she danced at. I was staying with my buddy Mike and this weirdo Chris dumped me for calls me on the phone and starts having a full blown conversation with me. He then tells me that if there was anything still left between Chris and I that he would step away. I found out later that night that they had gotten married! What a fucking weirdo! What was this idiot's m.o.? Later I would have the last laugh because that little weasel used to beat the shit out of her and they quickly got divorced. I hated Chris for what she did to me and was thrilled to find this entire thing out. Karma is a BITCH! I felt like I was in a vicious circle. I started to think, "Is all this crap really worth it to play guitar in a band?"

I then had the bright idea to start calling Gypsy. She said that she had really wanted to get out of Toronto and go to hair school somewhere. I suggested that she move to Florida and she could go to school down here and we could mend our relationship. When I told my mother about this she flipped!! She said "If you bring Gypsy down there I will be on a plane to Florida so fast that your head will spin!" So what did I do but book a flight for Gypsy. My mother was absolutely right. Gypsy flaked on me, and stiffed me for the plane ticket. I was pissed but wasn't shocked. I guess I'm a glutton for punishment. I didn't hear from Gypsy till three months later. She called me out of the blue to apologize. I was like "A little too late for that don't you think?" Gypsy then started calling me at eight in the morning every Sunday asking me if I could wire her money. Shit she even called my parents a few times. I knew then that Gypsy had turned into a junkie. My parents must have felt bad for her or something and gave her some money against my wishes. Funny, I never heard from her again.

   Things finally started to get better in my life. Kevin had moved into a new house and Brett and I moved into Kevin's old house. Around this time I met my best friend Lee. We were playing a benefit or something and after we did just a few songs we started hanging at the bar. This dude comes up to me and says, "Whatcha drinkin?" The more I talked to him I thought "This guy's nuts and he is right up my alley." Lee and I were inseparable. We would constantly get ourselves into the funniest and crazy predicaments. His dad was loaded and I mean loaded. He had this palatial mansion and was never there! Lee and I would have run of the house. We would bring all these girls back to the house and get hog wild in the Jacuzzi and the pool.

   I remember this one time we were all naked in his pool and we started to throw this Nerf football around. If you've ever done this you'll know that the ball becomes like a brick when water logged. Lee went running off the ledge and did the splits in the air and I nailed him right in the gizzard with that brick! I'll never forget the look on his face as he hit the water. There was never a dull moment with Lee and still isn't to this day. I remember coming home from a bar with Lee in his new Corvette. The street coming into my neighborhood had a sharp turn. Lee decides to take it doing 40 which wasn't that fast at all but the car caught some water and started to fishtail. All I could see was this guy's mailbox coming right for us. Lee was spinning the steering wheel like a top. We ended up doing a complete 180 into this guy's front yard. As we were spinning around I could see this guy's lawn coming up in pieces and covering the windshield of the 'Vette. I couldn't believe that nobody noticed a thing and we just sat there and laughed and then quietly drove off.

Roxx Gang After Show Party—
Vinnie, Me, Lee and Mike–'96

As I drove past the house the next day, it was totally evident that someone had spun out in his front yard. Like I said, never a dull moment with Lee.

Lee Markel: Stacey's Best Friend
I have known Stacey a long time and even though I never refer to him in this way, I have often thought of him as Stacey "Snake Eyes" Blades because he is always so close to his dreams and desires

only to have the rug pulled from under him at the last moment. I remember this time I offered to buy Stacey a guitar and he went out and found this choice Les Paul and called me so excited about it. I met him at the store a couple of days later and we went in to buy this killer Les Paul only to find out it was purchased earlier that day. He came up "Snake Eyes" again...

Back in '94 my sister got married and was now living in L.A. They had their first child, Clancy. I couldn't believe I was an uncle. Christmas of '97 I flew out to L.A. to spend the holidays with them and my parents. It was the first time my whole family was together since 1988! I was really excited to be going. I was meeting my nephew for the first time (he was already 3) and my brother-in-law. It was great to be back in L.A. I couldn't believe how much it had changed in the last eight years. My brother in law and I hit it off immediately and I thought I would drag him to the Rainbow. We got there early and parked ourselves in the main bar. It was a trip to be at the Bow again. I hadn't been there since '89! Within the first few minutes I had these two cute girls sitting across from DJ and I buying us drinks.

This one girl was definitely hitting on me but she was pounding drinks and pounding even more shots. An hour later she was sucking on my thumb and then passed out head first on the bar. DJ was having a blast and we talked with all kinds of interesting people. This guy had recognized me from Roxx Gang. He said "Let's cruise into the dining room, I want to introduce you to this Argentinean chick named Grace." We walked over to the corner dining room table. Grace had these crazy wolf eyes and looked a lot like Vanity. "Grace this is Stacey from Roxx Gang." She kind of did a double take and said in her South American accent "Oh Stacey, I have a picture of you and your band in my living room." My chances of picking her up were looking pretty good at this point. We sat and talked for an hour or so and I realized I had left DJ at the bar. DJ was having a blast and was digging having a rock n'roll brother in-law. Grace and I exchanged numbers and we made plans to hook up the next day. My sister drove me over the hill into Hollywood and I waited at this coffee shop for Grace. We shot the shit for a while and she asked if I wanted to come back to her place which was just a few blocks away on Whitley. I remember she didn't have too much furniture and we sat on the floor as she showed me all these magazines she was in, in Argentina. I guess Grace was popular in her home country. I ended up sleeping with her that afternoon. It had been a while and it was over very quickly, trust me. After a few hours we started up again and half way through my sister called me and told me that she was down the street and asked if I was ready to go. Dammit! I was just getting my swerve on and I had to get dressed and split.

My sister and DJ were living in this great house in Studio City and she was running her own furniture business and my brother-in-law was working for the city building the new subway line. They really had things great and I was very proud of her. However this was short lived and two years later they would be at each other's throats and moving to Utah. I went out to L.A. the next Christmas as well and met my niece for the first time. Wow I was an uncle again! She was only two weeks old at the time. She was so tiny and it was amazing to hold her in my arms. Clancy, who was 4 years old now, was stoked that he had a little baby sister but wasn't jealous at all. Most kids at that age act out because of the lack of attention.

My niece C.C and I—L.A. '97

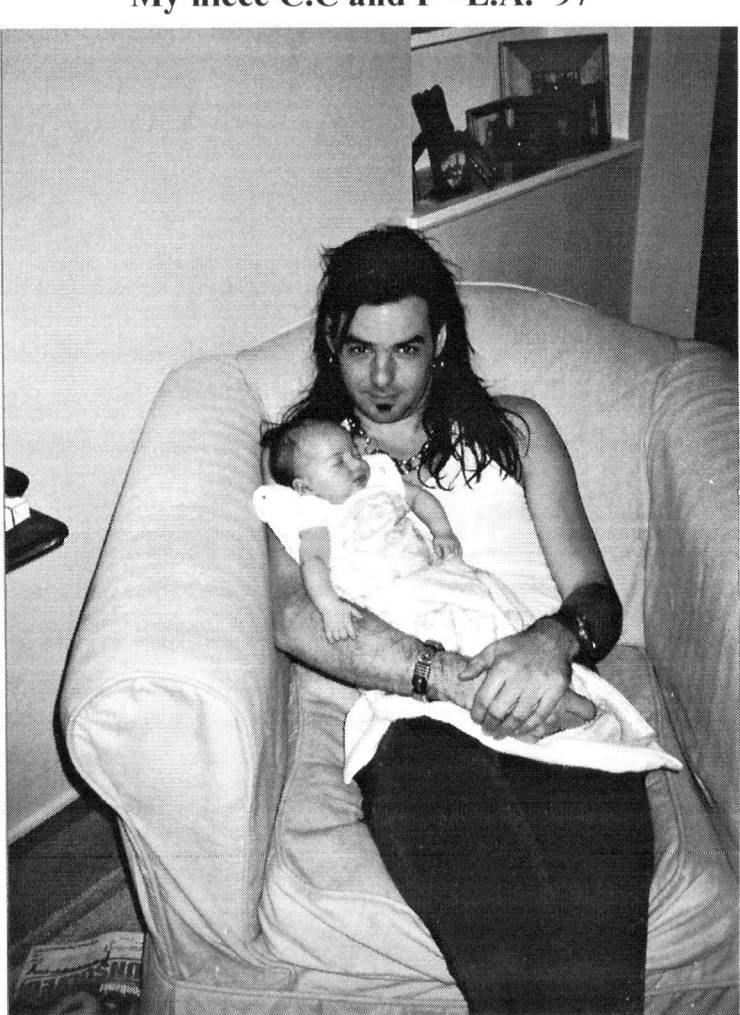

Roxx Gang was starting to work on a new album. I had suggested to Kevin earlier that year that we should go for that New York Dolls thing, you know the whole three chord bluesy punk rock. He said cool. Funny how two years later, Buckcherry came out with this kind of style and became hugely popular. So Kevin does the complete opposite and turns the band into this trippy bluesy psychedelic thing. Like T-Rex meets Muddy Waters. We had talked about renaming the band and going up to New York to showcase to labels. So Kevin comes up with this stupid name "Mojo Gurus" which he titled the record also. That fuckin record was the worst piece of shit I have ever been involved with in my music career. The Roxx Gang fans hated it and the critics panned it! Not only that but it sounded like shit. Kevin and Brett would cut so many corners if they could stash an extra buck in their wallets. The recording sessions were a nightmare. Why the hell would any one want to record an album in a house? They turned Brett's and my place upside down. There were cables everywhere, amps in closets and a makeshift control room in the third bedroom. Kevin was a prick the whole time we were making this record. I remember him flipping out at me for putting the microwave on while he was listening to a playback. That guy was such a dick and I wanted to punch his lights out!

We had added another guitar player earlier that year named Jeff. He was a funny guy but a bear to play with. I remember him and Vinnie the bass player would get into constant fights because Jeff would always be telling him how to play. If he wasn't doing it to Vinnie he would start on me. At this point I wanted to quit the band so bad but didn't have any other options at that time.

Surprisingly enough, we had gotten like 50 A&R responses from this press release Brett had sent out. I started thinking maybe we do have a shot at getting a deal after all. We set up a trip to New York City to do four showcase nights for seven labels. This wound Kevin up like a slingshot. He was so uptight about this thing going off without a hitch that he started to berate me and the rest of the band about our look, clothes and everything. He especially zeroed in on me. I think he said something like "You better not screw me out of a record deal dude! If you spike your hair I'm going to punch you in the face!" It took everything I had not to jump up and break every bone in that motherfucker's body! I really had gotten to the point of actually hating Kevin. The only reason I put up with him was because of the possibility of getting a deal.

We rented two vans, one passenger and one cargo van with all the gear. We decided to do the drive straight which took us about 22 hours, real fun. Either along the way or sometime before we left, I got pink eye. I was miserable all bloody week and I ended up getting it in both my eyes. I must have looked like a a heroin addict. We stayed at this huge Days Inn in Jersey right near the Lincoln Tunnel. Everyday we had to leave around 3 pm to get into the city because of the traffic. I was excited nevertheless because I thought there may been a good chance of getting a deal. Not only that but I was going too see my dear old friend Carolyn who I had basically grown up with. Carolyn and I had known each other since we were 9 years of age. We saw each other every week. Her parents and my parents were very good friends and we both went to the same church. Carolyn had moved to New York City

Partying Fools------Myself (with pinkeye), Tommy Weder, and Jeff Vitolo—NYC '98

when she was 17 to start her modeling career and I really hadn't seen her since! We had decided to hook up the first night in New York because we had that night off. Tommy and I took a cab into the city and went to this bar that Carolyn's boyfriend at the time owned. Tommy and I were there for like 45 minutes and I couldn't find her to save my life. Finally I saw her by the door and she had hardly aged at all! She still had the same youthful pretty face exactly like I remembered her having. I, on the other hand looked a little bit different.

Carolyn Haskell: Stacey's Childhood Friend

I was to meet Stacey at the Prohibition Bar in NYC. We hadn't seen each other for many years. I had been modeling abroad and I knew he had moved to Florida to join this band back in 92'. When he came into the bar my friend asked "How do you two know each other", we laughed, "we met in Sunday School." We used to hang out as kids in his basement when our parents went out to dinner and he would play guitar and say how he was going to be a rock star. He still plays me his new songs and coincidentally, we live 2 blocks from each other in L.A. Don't ever let him tell you that he doesn't play a mean "Away in a Manger."

We had fun hanging out and I don't think we paid for a drink all night. When Tommy and I got back to the hotel, the crew along with Jeff and our new bass player Vinnie were raising utter hell in my room. It looked like they had smoked ten joints and polished of a couple of bottles of Crown. I begged for them to leave because I really wanted to get some rest, but all they did was party harder. The next day those guys were fuckin hurtin' so bad. I remember our soundman Don lying on the floor of CBGB's by the sound booth during sound check. Needless to say Brett was pissed.

So we do the showcases and played well but nothing became of it. I think five or six labels showed up and probably walked out. I don't think Brett even spoke to any one of them. Like I had mentioned earlier, Brett was good at blowing smoke up peoples asses. I remember him telling us in the hotel room that this guy from Atlantic was coming out and had been wanting to sign a band just like us for the last year. I really believed that was a load of shit because no guy from Atlantic ever came and saw us in NYC.

A few nights after we got back from NYC, I was lounging around watching television and my phone rings, I say hello and I hear hello on the other line, I say hello again and I get this bitchy hello back. It was Christine, she somehow got my number. When I realized it was her I promptly said "What the fuck do you want!" There was dead silence on the other end. I think she was a little shocked to hear that from me. "Well I just called to apologize for treating you so badly. I guess I'm getting it back." I said "Oh really?" Like I said earlier, Chris had married this goofball who beat her up and treated her like shit. I said "well that's really too bad Chris." Of course I was grinning ear to ear on the other end of the phone. I hung up with her and a half an hour later there's a knock on my door. Sure enough when I opened up the door there was Chris. What the hell was with these girls! They would treat me like shit and months later come sniffing around my door. I guess the Blades tattoo does not wash off that easily.

Christine liked to do these impromptu pop-ins over at my place all the time. She would come by at the most inappropriate times like when I would be swimming in the pool with my girlfriend Angie or barbecuing with her and her kids. Anytime I saw that green teal Camaro of hers pull up to my house I would run for cover! I found myself always peering out the front window. I finally stopped answering the door and had to start screening my calls. I mean, what the hell did she want from me!

FIVE ROCK STAR THINGS NOT TO DO

1. Date Crazy Stripper

2. Fall in love with Crazy Stripper

3. Move in with Crazy Stripper

4. Take drugs in a frail emotional mental state

5. Give music lessons to a female fan:
   (She may just end up stalking your ass)

MISERY LOVES COMPANY

Chapter 7

Around this time the band's popularity locally was going quick. I mean I wasn't surprised. How many times can you go see the same thing over and over? Brett and Kevin used to turn down tours all the time. I just couldn't understand why these guys didn't want to work!

At the beginning of '97 I started to go out with this girl Angie. She actually went out with Dorian in the late 80's and subsequently had his daughter. She also had a 5 year old boy. Her kids were great and I enjoyed spending time with them. Angie and I dated off and on for about a year and a half. I fell madly in love with her and she was like a drug. Our chemistry was insane. Angie put up guards all the time and was the queen of bad decisions. I think she started realizing that I was not the right guy for her. She told me that I wasn't an appropriate father figure and that she couldn't handle the rock star lifestyle anymore. I guess in a way she was right. I did drag her into this crazy world of late night parties, concerts, drugs and alcohol. She seemed to be having the time of her life, but she had other plans for me. Angie dumped me on Valentine's Day and broke my heart. Why is it every time

I breakup with a chick she makes a concerted effort to fuck with me? She would still call me after we broke up and would show up at Kevin's girlfriend's hair salon. Of course I would have to hear all about it the next day. I told Kevin's girlfriend not to take her calls anymore which she agreed. Of course she didn't and felt it was more important to book a $40 hair appointment than respect my wishes to stay away from Angie.

Kevin and his girlfriend felt they needed to boss and govern everybody. They would lecture me like parents sometimes. I was like "Fuckoff and mind your own business." My fucked up life was boiling over. The only saving grace was my job. I had started working at another vacation place and my boss took a liking to me and promoted me to a manager. I was in charge of about 12 people. It was very stressful at times but I actually enjoyed it and I was a pretty damn good manager. I was making really good money off all the vacation sales my reps would do. I remember at one point making $1000 dollars a week and only working 30 to 35 hours a week.

A light bulb went off: "L.A. Moving Fund"

I was making such good money that I was able to save about $1500 to $2000 a month. So here we are doing another record, at least this one was rocking. Funny how I hardly saw any money from these albums. I was convinced that these monies were going elsewhere other than mine and the rest of my band mates' pockets. Every time Tommy, Jeff and I would ask Brett about our money, he would instantly turn red and his eyes would start darting back and forth. He might as well have had a flashing guilty sign on his forehead. After we recorded *"Smokin TNT and Drinkin Dynamite"* in '98, we went to NYC to showcase again under the name Mojo Gurus. There was some really good songs on that album but I knew nothing was going to become of this trip and this was my last ditch effort for this band. At least this time we were flying into NYC and the poor crew had to drive all the way with the gear. Jet Blue Airlines had just come out and the flight crew was a riot on that flight, they were giving us all kinds of free drinks and were practically partying with us.

We only had three labels come out and they all passed, big surprise. I think everybody had pretty much given up on the idea of getting a deal. We had this song on S.T.D.D. called *"Star Trip."* It was a really cool song and very Kid Rock like. We decided to shoot a video for that song. We rounded up all these dancers and shot over a two or three day period. The video came out really cool and once again, Christian Moriarty did a fantastic job on it. I had gotten kind of chummy with this one girl in the video. She was this really pretty brunette that looked a little like Lara Flynn Boyle. She came by my house a few days later to watch some raw footage of the video. I went out with her just a few times and she was a really weird chick, which of course made me want her more. I remember I went back to her place one night and walked in her pad and was mortified. Her daughter, who was maybe 8 or 9, was sleeping all by herself on the couch. There was cat food everywhere, clothes scattered around the whole apartment, big piss stains from her cat on the carpet and Cheerios all over the kitchen floor. I was so disgusted I instantly split, and needless to say never took her calls again.

Getting back to the song "*Star Trip*", I remember our entertainment lawyer coming into the dressing room after we played one showcase night in New York and said "Great job guys, really good show, you really got the hit song with Star Trap." This guy was shopping a deal for us and doesn't even know the name of the song! That was really reassuring to hear.

We did a Roxx Gang show the last night we were in New York in Queens and I think 20 people showed up. To me it was no surprise and I could've cared less. In my mind I had already quit.

A few months after we got back from that NYC trip, things got really bad in the band. All Kevin wanted to do was learn old blues tunes and work them up. Then he made us start opening up for ourselves as the Mojo Gurus when we played a Roxx Gang show. I had reached my boiling point and going to rehearsal was like going to the dentist for a root canal. At rehearsal one afternoon Kevin was trying to force one of those stupid old songs on us and I said "Why don't we work on an original instead." He got all shitty and said "Well you got one!!!" As soon as he turned around I double flipped him off in front of the whole band.

I had to mask this anger and depression somehow. My buddy

Frank who lived right down the street had delved into the dark world of cocaine and sucked me willingly into it. I was stuck in Florida and wanted out of this band so bad. Frank got really fucked up on blow. He would call me every other day and say "I got bunny trails get your ass over here." One afternoon Frank had gotten an eight ball and we decided to throw a party. Vinnie and his girlfriend came by and Lee and his buddy also stopped in for the festivities. We must have chopped out 20 caterpillar lines and had a case of Budweiser in the fridge. After a few hours of coke babble and downing beers, Vinnie had to meet up with this guitar tech that used to work for us. Our old tech must have given Vinnie a monster line of blow and when Vinnie walked back into Frank's he looked like he had seen a poltergeist and was sweating profusely. It kind of freaked us all out because he could've very well OD'd. Vinnie was actually freaking out and I thought his heart was going to explode. He went into the bathroom and puked his guts out. After that he came right back to the table and slugged a beer. I was like hell yea! Now we're partying! My band mate and friend almost went into a coke induced coma and I starting chopping another line out for him. At this point in the night we were all completely out of our heads. I thought to myself "Let's get even more stupid." And so the

Frank Kenny: Stacey's friend and old drug partner

Me and Stacey met around 1997 and became friends. Soon after, he moved in to my place and the adventure began. We tore up the town together for the next two or three years not to mention a few chicks

as well. There was one night I remember, we had been hanging out at my house after picking up a couple of 8 balls and a few friends stopped by and the party began. Stacey's boy Lee came by with a buddy of his and a bottle of vodka that had only a short time to live around us. When Vinnie Granese and his girl Rhonda got there we were snorting lines the size of my finger. Vinnie had stepped outside to meet a friend of his when he came back in he was white as a sheet and whacked out of his head. He said he just did the biggest line of his life out there and thought he was gonna OD. He spent the next hour or so kneeling over the toilet till he finally came around. After that we were sitting at the table when Lee mumbled something and began to chug down the rest of the bottle. Well that pretty much finished him off and he wound up passing out in the bathtub puking his guts up.

One time we celebrated Stacey's birthday at a club in St Petersburg called Butious Maximus, sneaking outside to do lines in the car whenever we could. As usual I bet we did thousands of dollars worth of that shit over those couple of years if not more. It is all still pretty hazy to me but I know there's no doubt we always had a blast. I was bummed when he left for L.A. but it was what he was meant to do. He belonged out there and well look at him now. He will always be one of my best friends we still talk regularly and I see him whenever he comes to town with the Guns, granted I think we have both mellowed although just a little with age.

drinking games began. I told Lee to grab a bottle of vodka out of the pantry, and informed everyone we were going to do shots and choppers. Basically it was stupid: you snorted a line and banged a shot of straight vodka. Lee however had decided he was going to take it up a notch, and after he did a line, he grabbed the whole bottle and goes "This is how you do it Bay-bee!" Lee tilted the bottle back and let 'er rip! After he put the bottle back on the table, it must have hit him all at once and he looked at me and made the most funny, fucked up face I had ever seen! He was fucked and knew it. He spent the rest of the night passed out with his head in the toilet. It didn't phase us at all and we just kept

partying. His poor friend was completely sober and couldn't move Lee to save his life. After six months of snorting blow I realized if I didn't stop, Frank would be desolate or dead and I was slowly turning into an addict. Crawling along a white tile floor looking for specs of coke at the end of the night was getting old. We had one last blowout and I mean blowout on New Years Eve. Cocaine is an evil drug that will suck your soul out.

That same year, there were these two girls that came to my work one day, Lisa and Lora. The two L's. These two were big hitters in the "Vacation Sales" world. I thought they were both cute too. Lora started to manage the nightshift but she would be in my office a lot during the day. I got to know both of them very well and they became good friends and we starting hanging out a lot. I started to notice that Lora was flirting with me big time.

I kind of blew her off because we were both managers at the same company.

Lisa Grollino: Stacey's Ex-Wife
I can clearly remember the first time I saw Stacey. It was at a Roxx Gang show in FL way back in early 1998. It was at this place called Gasoline Alley and I can remember the local rock radio station really plugging the show. So my friend & I decided to go. The place was packed and the band hit the stage with so much energy! We weren't able to get close to the stage, but I had a great view of Stacey. I still vividly remember what he was wearing: floppy cap, black velvet jacket with no shirt. He just looked so good, played awesome and I was fixated on him the whole night. The thing that's kind of weird now, is that while watching him on stage, I kept thinking, "Wow, this guy totally looks like a combination of Phil Lewis and Tracii Guns". He really did look like he'd just stepped off the L.A. Guns bus. We had to leave before the band was done, so I didn't get to meet Stacey that night.

July 1998. About six months after I'd first seen Stace live. My friend & I started a new job together at this travel office and (of course) are immediately drawn to the only long haired rocker looking guy in the place. (Two of us, one of him – this would later present a problem). We didn't recognize him right away, but we got to know him and we all became good friends (for a while). He & I had so much in common including the complete same taste in music. One night we were up 'til like 3:00 a.m. just talking and looking at all these old music magazines I had and the L.A. Guns thing came up again. I told him, "You know, you look like you should be playing L.A. Guns"! He said how they've always been one of his favorite bands. Not long after that, we went to see L.A. Guns live. We all had a blast that night! It's kind of weird thinking back on it now, but who would've thought: not only would Stacey & I get married, we'd move to Los Angeles and he'd actually be playing in L.A. Guns! He definitely had to work his way there and is one of the most dedicated, determined musicians I've ever known!

Don't stick your pen in the company ink right! The more I withdrew the more Lora would chase after me. I finally gave in and started to date her. MISTAKE! You'd think I would have learned by now and this had disaster written all over it. Lora was a total bitch and manipulated me every chance she got. We only went out for a few months and grew to hate each other. By this time I had really started to get close to Lisa. Funny, I would see the things Lora did to Lisa and be like "How can you let that bitch get away with treating you like that!" Lora and Lisa lived together as well.

Lisa Grollino:
Stacey, Lora & I had become really good friends and started hanging out quite a bit. This one night we all went out drinking and ended up back at our place. We continued drinking and then decided to play Truth or Dare which somehow led to Strip Poker (Stacey's idea). Lora & I were sober enough to decide together we weren't stripping that night. We figured out a way to cheat without having to remove too much. He had no clue and we concluded later that he just wanted to take his clothes off.

After I stopped seeing Lora a switch had turned off in me. I think I finally snapped. I was so jaded and cynical from all these abusive and twisted relationships. Lisa and I would start dating but not for long. I was so fucked up inside that I just couldn't handle another girlfriend. By this time I think Brett wanted to be on his own. I think he told me that he and Kevin were going to sell the house because they were broke or something. Of course they never did. I smelled a rat. Brett and I were tight but he seemed to be distancing himself from me around this time.

I ended up moving in with Frank. He had a much nicer and bigger house. Plus he had a pool and Jacuzzi. Frank would fall off the wagon from time to time and start doing blow again. I refused to partake. I knew that if I started that shit again, it would lead me into a downward spiral. I'll never forget coming home one afternoon and Frank was lit up like the 4th of July. As I was pulling my Camaro into the garage he burst through the door like "Kramer" and started directing me like one of those guys directing an airliner into the gate on the tarmac. What made it even funnier is that there was a big snotty white line bleeding out of his nose.

Frank eventually got back with his twisted ex-girlfriend. This chick put him through the wringer and Frank was a different person around her. She treated him like shit! Frank then had the bright idea to move her back into the house. Well, I guess I was on my way out. I started looking for my own place. I looked at so many shitholes. I didn't want to spend a lot of money because it would have ruined my "L.A. Moving Fund."

Lisa had just bought this cool little house in St. Pete. I ended up moving in there and it was great. By this time I started to get addicted to getting tattooed. It was something that really made me feel special and alive. I met this killer artist named Jeff that worked at this shop right beside Gasoline Alley (Clearwater's local rock club). We would finish a tat and then pop over to the Alley for a beer. Shit, I was at that damn tattoo shop every week for like two months. Lisa actually got me a gift certificate from Wildside Tattoos for Christmas. Jeff got a kick out of me being so into getting tattooed that when Lisa went in to get the gift certificate he said "Lisa, why don't I just sell you a tattoo needle and you can fill it with water and run it all over his body." I still laugh about this to this day and I actually contemplated it for a minute, just kidding.

Wildside Tattoos—Clearwater, Florida---'98

I knew Lisa had feelings for me still, and I was starting to come around and was feeling the same way. She was a great girl with a heart of gold and I ended up marrying her. I said to her one day "Hey, you want to take a trip to L.A.?" She had never been so she was like "Yeah totally." We got a good deal on a flight and hotel and of course rented a bad ass Mustang to drive around in for the week. I couldn't believe how much L.A. had picked up since the late 90's. The scene was busting and there was something going on there every night of the week. I started to suggest to Lisa how she would feel about moving here. Three months later we got married and decided to sell the house and move to L.A. I felt like my life was finally going in the right direction.

A few months before we left, I had started taking Sudafed for my allergies. Sudafed contains sudephedrine, which they make speed from. Little did I know I was becoming addicted to these pills. I started to take about ten of them a day. That shit fucked up my prostate so bad that I developed prostatitis, which is an infection in the prostate gland. No fun let me tell you. I was pissing out this stuff that looked like thick yellow Kool-aid. I went to the doctor and got treated, but my prostate has never been the same. I was in agony and had to go to a urologist. He told me that he wanted to do a cyscoptopy. He really didn't elude to what that procedure was and if he had, I would have went running for the door! Basically, they numb your dick and shove a tube all the way up your urethra to your insides. The tube contains a camera so they can look at your plumbing. It was the worst experience of my life. Fuck did that shit hurt! Not only that but because of the pressure, your urethra gets all scraped up and when you have to pee it feels like your pissing out shrapnel.

I eventually got better and couldn't wait to tell the band and Kevin to fuckoff. Finally I was leaving! I had been pretty sick over the last few weeks and made those guys cancel a bunch of shows. I told Kevin I needed a break and he got kind of pissy with me and replied "See ya!" Little did he know that I would pull the wool over his eyes and just bolt when I moved two weeks later. I exacted my revenge like a true Scorpio. Those guys didn't know shit and were completely stumped when I left. Maybe if Kevin had treated me with a little more respect over the years instead of brow beating me, I would have nicely told him I was leaving the band.

Lisa and I started to plan our wedding and our move to L.A. I had already started to work on putting a new band together for my arrival in L.A. I put an ad in the *Recycler* and one of the first people to call me was Eric Stacy, former Faster Pussycat bassist. Eric and I hit it off pretty quick. We wanted to start a band like Buckcherry, Turbo Negro and Backyard Babies. I told him that I would there in a few weeks and we would hit it full throttle.

Lisa and I were married on June 30th, 2001. My parents and my sister flew down for the wedding and it was a small ceremony with about 25 to 30 people. Lisa has a big family, practically most of the wedding party was her side of the family. I only had about five friends come.

Our boss Jim, his buddy Matt and Lee took me out the night

before for my bachelor party. We had a blast and hit a few strip joints and ended up at the Dollhouse. I was trashed by the end of the night and passed out in my bed with all my clothes still on! My Dad came by at three in the afternoon to get me and I was still in bed. I was totally hung over and grabbed my tux and a few other things and headed off to their hotel. "Holy shit I'm getting married today!" I was nervous as hell. The ceremony went off without a hitch and when Lisa and I were reciting our vow's she looked like she was going to shit a gold brick. I guess she was nervous too!

The reception was held at Lisa's parent's house in Treasure Island. Lisa's dad cooked the food for the entire wedding. That man is a master in the kitchen. We had a fun day until my sister got hammered and was pissing off my parents. Never a dull moment in my family and this still is true to this day.

Lisa and I Wedding Party--- June 30th 2001

A week later, Lisa and I sold the house and put a U-Haul trailer on the back of her car and loaded it up with all our shit. I had sold my Camaro and was sad to see my Z-28 go bye- bye. I had some great times with that car. We hit the road around 6 am and drove till we reached Louisiana. I had driven like 11 hours and we could not find a vacant hotel to save our lives. The drive was interesting to say the least. One night in San Antonio we stayed at this shithole off the 10 Freeway. I went to the convenience store across the street to get some beer and on the way back this weird old guy starts to push this KKK propaganda on me. Two and a half days later we arrived in L.A. Driving across America is no fun let me tell you and if you have a big trailer behind you, it's even worse. You could never go past 75 miles an hour because if you did the trailer would start fishtailing. I couldn't wait to dump that fuckin thing. The first week we were there, was a pain in the ass. I must have gotten three parking tickets in the first two days and it actually took us about nine days to find a bloody apartment! Once we moved in and got furniture we both took a deep breath for the first time in weeks.

THE CITY OF ANGELS

Chapter 8

Eric Stacey and I met for the first time and started to put the band together. I remember this funny scenario when we played phone tag for a week before I left for L.A. One day, he left me a message.

"Dude, I got the name of the band. I don't want to tell you on the machine so call me back," he said. When I returned his call, I got his answering machine. He called me later but I wasn't home.

"I really love the name we came up with… it's Supercool!" he said on the recording.

I listened to his message and gave him a ring. But I got his damn machine again.

"I'm sure the name is Supercool, but tell me what the hell it is!" I screamed into the tape.

"Hey bro, the name is Supercool," he said in yet another message.

I called him yet another time and my heart sank as I heard his now familiar greeting on the answering machine.

"Look, Eric. I know the name is cool. But I can't take this teasing anymore. What the hell is it?"

He finally reached me on the phone and we were able to speak directly.

"That's the name," he said. "The name of the band is Supercool."

I was like o-k-a-y? I hated it from the get go but I was so happy to be out of Roxx Gang, I didn't care. I was really getting excited to leave all this crap in Florida behind me and start my life over, so to speak.

Eric had found this great, young, tattooed singer/guitarist named Lantz L'amour. We started to write together and it felt great to play with some other cats. We searched and searched for a drummer and finally nabbed Vikk Foxx. Vikk was in Enuff Z Nuff and had also played in Vince Neil's band. He was a smoking drummer and made us sound great. After three months together we had recorded a six song EP called *"Live At the Wilcox Hotel"* and we were heading off to Japan for five dates in Tokyo. I was stoked and had always wanted to go to Japan. It was a long flight and Vikk and I started to drink Bloody Marys. We must have polished off a few too many because they cut us off after about 10 or 12 of them. I remember the Head Steward saying to me (insert Japanese accent) "We are flying at very high altitude sir and those drinks have gone to your head." I said "No shit Sherlock, fix me up with another round!" I think I passed out after that. So we finally land and the promoters picked us up at the Narita Airport. I was feeling a little whacked from the flight and the time change. We were staying in Shinjuku, right in the heart of Toyko.

I remember when Vikk and I walked into our hotel room, we were like, "You've got to be kidding me"! It was the size of a shoebox! Vikk actually persuaded the clerk to give us another "bigger room," and trust me it wasn't that much bigger. We all got settled and went out for a bite to eat.

It was amazing to be in Tokyo. I must have been snapping off shots from my camera every five seconds. By 8 o'clock I was fried (it was probably 5 in the morning L.A. time). We went back to the hotel and crashed. Of course by six in the morning I was wide awake! Japan is a tough one to adjust to time wise. The shows went great and we really had a good time there. The fans in Japan are absolutely amazing! Any musician who's toured there will tell you. They follow you around and shower you with gifts. I remember some very funny moments from that tour. One afternoon we were coming out of sound check and there was like this intense rainstorm that might as well have been a Category 5 Hurricane. We had to go maybe 30 feet from the club to the van. I ran for it first. Everyone was laughing because the harder I ran the more the wind would push me back. When I got to the car I was fuckin drenched. I must have looked like a drowned rat cause Eric and Lantz started calling me "Splinter" (He was the rat that died from pneumonia in the *Teenage Mutant Ninja Turtles Movie*). Vikk had tried to open an umbrella in that wind and it turned that thing inside out so quickly and snapped it like a twig. We were all soaking wet and laughing our asses off.

Vikk had resoled his boots before we left and must have not

been used to the new heels he put on. There was like two or three times he pulled a complete "Kramer" from *Seinfeld* move and wiped out on his ass. The funniest was outside of Denny's. He's just standing on the steps and all the sudden his legs are in two different directions and he's toppling down the concrete steps like a bag of potatoes.

Eric knew this girl that worked at this huge bootleg video store called 'Airs Video." This place was amazing! Any band you could think of they had it! I even picked up a live Roxx Gang concert from '94. This girl Junko who managed the place let us have three videos each at no charge. One night in Roppongi on our way to the Lexington Queen (Tokyo's version of the Rainbow), I noticed I had been taking a ton of pictures and thought no way there is there this many exposures on the film. I opened up the camera and gasped! There was no fuckin film in that thing. I flipped. All those great pictures I had taken all week were nothing! I remember I had asked my wife to put film in the camera and she must have spaced it. I bought some film the last day and must have shot a whole roll in a matter of a couple hours.

So, back to the night at the Lexington Queen. It was an interesting night to say the least. There are all these American models, male and female that would hang out there. It's a lot like an L.A. bar, full of fakes, flakes and pushers. I remember this American guy who was a real estate mogul trying to push this 13-year-old Saigon chick onto Lantz.

Supercool—Tokyo, Japan
'02 -- L to R: Stacey, Eric, Lantz and Vikk

The night after that we went to this bar called Mothers. The place was the size of my living room and they blasted hard rock and metal. It was so loud in there and you couldn't see a damn thing. They had all these mirrors on the walls and it looked like there was another room. I was like, "Hey Lantz, lets check this other room out," we then proceeded to both walk completely into the wall at the same time. I remember I was in rare form that night and was dancing on top of my bar stool to Offspring's "Separated." The last night the promoters took us out for a farewell traditional Japanese meal. It was awesome, we took off our shoes and sat on the floor while we ate sushi and drank for hours.

We came back from that tour and the band just completely fell apart. Let's just say there was so much dysfunction going on I just couldn't deal with it anymore.

Not long after Supercool broke up I started working part time doing extra work for television shows. That job sucked, it was like being a sheep herded back and forth. I did the typical "Audience" work and sat through endless hours of stupid game shows and talk shows. "*Talk Soap*" had to be the worst. The pay sucked and you spent hours sitting around with a bunch of weirdos. One show however worked out pretty cool. VH1 had a show called "*Late Nite with Zack*." I ended up getting in the first two rows of that particular taping and got some camera time. One of the guests on this particular episode was psychic Gary Spivey. The host Zach would come into the audience and have people ask Gary some psychic predictions. Zach actually came over to me and said,

"What's your name?" I said of course Stacey and he blurts out "What's your question miss?" As the audience cracked up, I asked Gary "where do you see my career in the next year?" Gary replies "I see you doing something over in Europe in the next year or so". I thought, this guy is full of shit. Funny almost exactly a year later I was in Europe touring. Coincidence?

Lantz and I decided to pick up the pieces and start another band. All these new rock bands were coming out of the woodwork and getting signed. We wanted to put something together that was like street punk rock but with a pop edge. I thought "Well this is my last shot at making it so to speak, so it's all or nothing." Lantz and I had written some amazing songs, stuff that I thought had a real chance at getting a deal. We recruited our buddy Jamie on bass. For the life off us we couldn't find a drummer so we had our buddy Pat Muzingo from Junkyard fill in. Pat just ended up staying in the band. I plotted every move with this band and came up with the perfect way to shop a deal. The guys kept second guessing me, but I proved them wrong when 26 labels responded to our mail out.

S.M.A.C.K, I thought, had a real fighting chance. We smoked live and had some radio ready songs, (I might as well have that saying on my tombstone). The labels didn't think so and rejected us across the board. However there was still a chance. Nancy Walker at Island liked our stuff enough that she wanted to hear more material. I begged the rest of the guys to get back into the studio to record these killer new songs we had. But it was too late, the band was already starting to crack. I had driven these guys so hard that they were ready to kill me! I think I was so desperate to make it that I just had blinders on the whole time. Playing the local scene and shopping a deal had just sucked everybody's soul out including mine. I could hear the anthem "TAPS" playing in my head as the band announced that this was our last show.

Jamie Zimlin: Ex-Smack Bassist
Since I met Stacey Blades in 2001, I felt like I found a great friend, musical soul mate, and all around good man. Through death, marriage, divorce, break ups, and other unnecessary Hollywood drama, I have had him as a trusted friend by my side. He is fiercely loyal to his friends and band mates, has a great sense of humor, and a uncanny knack for random trivia. I will always be grateful to have him as one of my closest friends. However, Stacey's drive for stardom was one of the main causes of our band's demise among other things. His over zealousness in trying to procure a record deal ultimately caused our untimely end. Luckily for us, we all still remain close friends. I one day hope to have the honor toplay in a band with him again. His talent and drive are second to none.

I felt like I had been shot out of a spaceship. I had spent practically my whole life trying to make it musically from the ground up. I went from one band to starting another and another. I had spent eight years of my 20's and early 30's in Roxx Gang thinking that was my meal ticket and all that gig left me was a twitch in my left eye. Well that "Force" that had been holding me back all those years finally won and I succumbed to it. It flipped me out; all that sacrificing and hard work didn't amount to shit. I thought, "Dammit it's just not fair!" However every cloud has its silver lining so to speak.

Right after Smack broke up I got a call from my friend Keff. He said that L.A.Guns was looking for a guitar player. I said what happened to Tracii? He told me he wasn't coming back to the band (Tracii permanently left to do Brides of Destruction with Nikki Sixx) and asked if I was interested. I was like HELL YA! Keff was friends with Phil Lewis the singer of L.A. Guns and set up a lunch date to meet. We went to the French Quarter restaurant on Santa Monica Blvd. It was really cool meeting Phil. He was a true British Rock Star in my books. I had met him one time before at the Dragonfly but I think he was kind of fucked up. While we ate lunch, Phil talked about how they were scheduled to do a cover record and they also had a full European tour in the works. We finished our meals and went over to Phil's place. I brought some old Roxx Gang cds to show Phil I could really play. Steve Riley the drummer came by Phil's and It was a trip to meet him, I mean I was a big WASP fan.

The following week, Steve called me and set up a rehearsal slash audition. I learned about six or seven songs. I felt like that 23 year old again preparing for the Roxx Gang audition except this was way bigger. I headed up to North Hollywood to their rehearsal studio and it was a cold, crappy, rainy day. I started shooting the shit with everybody and met bassist Adam Hamilton for the first time. Adam was one of the sweetest, funniest musicians I have ever met. We are both Scorpios so of course we hit it off right away.

We started the audition off with *"Sex Action"* and *"Kiss My Love Goodbye."* I really gelled with the band and felt insane chemistry right from the first power chord. After that second song Phil came over and hugged me. I felt all that shit over the last 15 years melt away. We played a few more songs like "*Electric Gypsy*", "*One more Reason*" and "*Ballad* of *Jayne*." It tripped me out, all those songs I had worn out on my record player so many years ago, I was now playing with the band. Phil and Brad, the Tour Manager at the time, said "Are you ready to go to Europe?" Tough answer there.

Steve Riley: L.A. Guns Drummer

Phil and I were starting to think it was going to be difficult to find a permanent replacement for Tracii. After all we used six to seven different guys up to the time we met Stacey. An old friend, Keff Radcliffe, introduced us over at Phil's place. Right off the bat we knew Stace had it together. He was a fan of the band and was from the same school as us. After one rehearsal we were ready to do a show. Stacey had learned the whole set and was real faithful to the way he played it. Staying really close to the original recordings, yet adding his own flavor to it. We wanted someone who was in for the long ride. Phil and I are lifers in this business and it was important to find someone who felt the same as we do.

I drove home with a perma grin on my face. I walked in the door and looked at my wife and said, "I'm going to Europe and I got the gig!" Lisa was stoked, but had this look of pleasant uncertainty. I think she knew our lives were not going to be the same from that point on. When I joined L.A. Guns I was basically thrown into the deep end. We went immediately into pre-production for the cover record. I had to learn 12 or 13 covers for the album and then we were leaving a month later for the tour which means I had to learn about 16 LAG tunes.

Adam Hamilton: *Friend and Former LA Guns Bassist*
We had been pulling our hair out trying to find the guy after a series of colorful characters had come and gone in a short period of time. I knew in my heart Tracii had no real intention of returning once he was ensconced in "Nikki's World" I saw it coming a mile away. But, when after Chris Holmes, Brent Muscat, and Kerri Kelli all came and went I have to be honest, I was having my doubts as to whether things were going to work out or not. I just didn't know anybody who had what it would take for things to really change. What I had been convinced of was that even with Tracii gone, most people didn't care. They just wanted to hear those songs and hear them sung by Phil. I knew I was in it for the long haul and something would pan out. It just had to. Keff, being the stand up guy that he is, called Phil and said that he might have someone for the gig. Knowing Keff well enough, we knew it had to be serious and we got excited at the possibility that we might have our guy even though we had not met him yet. When he said that his friend had at one time played in Roxx Gang, I got even more curious.

We scheduled a rehearsal and picked some songs to jam on. From the moment Stacey walked into the room I just had a sense that he was the guy. He looked great, like he was already in the band. Stacey seemed really cool and friendly. He pulled out a Les Paul and slung it low. We played a few notes and I just knew that he was in. I could tell this was a guy, like me, who was so excited about the gig and would give it his all. Little did I know that he would become like a brother and would keep us in stitches with his comedic skits and impersonations. My life changed when I joined the Guns and I got to see the same thing happen when Stacey began experiencing the same thing. Getting to travel the world and play rock and roll with a true great rock and roll band and to do it with someone so positive and excited was amazing.

My head was spinning, (careful what you wish for right) especially when they told me Andy Johns was producing the record. Andy is one of the biggest legendary producers out there. His credentials are second to none. I remember the first time Andy came to the rehearsal studio. I was like holy shit, this guy produced the Stones, Zeppelin, Rod Stewart and Van Halen! We entered the studio a few weeks later. The record went pretty well and I was really gelling with the band. Looking back on it I was wound up so tight that I think I could have let loose a little more on it. Overall I think it came out pretty good. Oh and it felt good to be fuckin paid for a change.

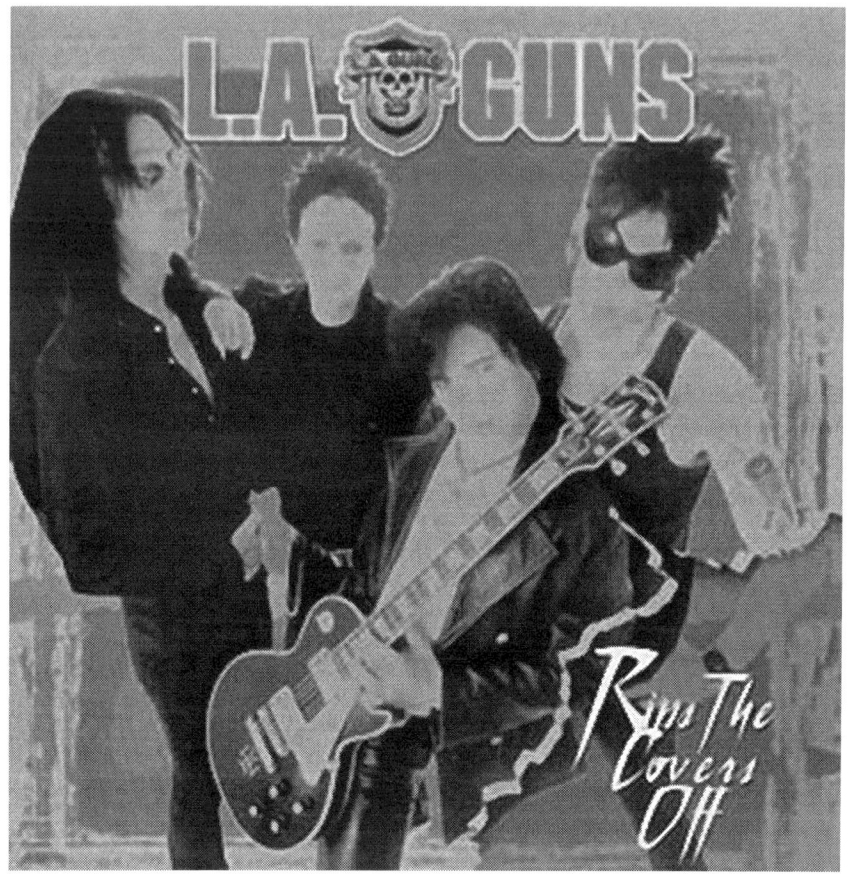

I remember that spring Adam and I were hanging out with Nikki Sixx at Clown Studios in Santa Monica. Nikki was looking over the new album and asking me questions. It fuckin blew my mind! Here I was, having a conversation with Sixx about an album I just did with L.A. Guns. Anyways we went back into rehearsals for the European tour. I remember Steve not wanting to rehearse, I was like "Are you fucking kidding me!" No way dude! I think he was having some fun with me.

We were scheduled to do about four weeks in Europe. We were going to Italy, Germany, Austria, Switzerland, Norway, Sweden, and the U.K. I was busting and stoked not only to see Europe but play all the great L.A. Guns songs live. We flew to Heathrow and picked up this utter piece of shit double decker tour bus called the 'Liberty.' I had to earn my sea legs and this tour was definitely my initiation into the band. It was February and it was freezing in Europe. That bus was like a fishing lodge on wheels. Nothing worked, it smelled like diesel and the bunks were like coffins. The first show was amazing and I was nervous as hell! I had tweaked my back out and probably looked like a stiff piece of wood up there. The fans were going crazy and the meet and greet was insane. There were a few people with Roxx Gang CD's and I was pleasantly surprised! Later that night on the bus, I was going from the top area of the bus to the bottom lounge. The bus had this death trap stairway. My shoe hit some water and I was airborne. I landed on the bottom step with my back ribs absorbing the fall. I fuckin saw stars! There was that force lurking around the corner. It could have been a lot worse; I could have broken my wrist or something.

The third or fourth day into the tour we were in Torrino, Italy. I was coming off the bus and this guy stopped dead in his tracks and goes "Ah Stacey Blades froma Roxxa Gang. I cannota believe it, pincha me I'ma dreamin." I was cracking up on the inside but it felt really good to get some recognition for a change. The Europeans are very serious about their rock n' roll. They know every song, album and everything there is to know about you!

Brad, the tour manager at the time, really fucked with me the whole tour. He figured that this was my hazing period and put me through hell. I thought to myself "Is this guy for real?" Brad stopped working for us after a while. He had been with the band for a long time and I think it became just too stressful for him. Fuck that guy would be yelling 24-7. I'm surprised he didn't give himself a heart attack! Deep down Brad was a good guy, but felt he needed to be a general all the time.

That fuckin bus got the better of everybody. It was so cold on that damn thing and there was no central heat. We had to use a space heater in the bunk area and you could forget about hanging in the bottom lounge 'cause it was like a meat locker. At night you would have to climb into that tiny bunk with a ski cap, scarf and long underwear 'cause it was so cold. Then of course three hours later you would wake up soaking wet from all the clothing layers. I couldn't sleep in those tiny bunks anymore so I started sleeping in the front lounge. That wasn't much better since the driver was below me. I think he used to be a miner or something because he would be coughing and hacking all through the night while he was lighting up cigarettes as he muttered in his thick Manchester accent "Bloody Fukin Hewll." The Swiss Alps were spectacular and Stockholm was amazing. I remember the skies in Sweden were just out of this world. We played this really weird place in Berlin. It was one of the most bizarre gigs I have ever played. I think the place was a gay metal biker bar. It was called Halford's and it had a giant 30 foot statue of Rob Halford in it. The gig totally sucked! I think the staff really had it in for us and didn't promote the show worth a shit. There was like 30 people there and there were all these dudes that looked like a German basketball team.

After Germany we were heading to Sweden. We had take the bus up to Northern Germany and then had to take a ferry over to Sweden. We all ate breakfast on the ferry and I think Adam had eaten a pink sausage. Adam and I had our own little state room on the ferry. It was a pretty long ride up to Sweden. As we were about to dock, Adam didn't look well at all. He was sitting on this little bench by the door. He was complaining that he couldn't sleep the whole ride. I said "Why don't you take a Xanax so you can sleep." I barely got the last word out and Adam turned green with a look of horror in his eyes and darted toward the bathroom and projectile vomited at least 12 feet. He sprayed the entire bathroom. I felt bad for him but busted out laughing. The poor guy must have had food poisoning because over the next 24 hours all he did was puke and shit. Being on that horrible bus didn't help either.

The Sweden shows were really good and when we played in Stockholm the place went mental. It reminded me off a Sex Pistols show. I remember Brad being sucked into this vortex of people at one point. The look on that's guys face was priceless! After Sweden we headed over to do a show in Oslo, Norway. Oslo looked a lot like Moscow, and there were so many beautiful women. I remember this one dude in the audience was all glammed out and looked like Kris Kattan's famous SNL character "Mango." It was so endearing to watch this guy try to mouth the words to *"Long Time Dead."*

After the Norway stop we were heading off to the U.K. We were going to take a ferry ride for 13 hours. However we never made the ferry and either someone in the crew or the bus driver fucked up on the ferry times and we missed it! When Riley found this out he hit the roof! We were playing the next night in Sheffield. We basically had to drive 20 hours from Norway to make the gig. Because of Coach Laws, a bus driver cannot drive more than 9 or 10 hours. We had to fly 2 other drivers in so they could split the shifts up. It was a pain in the ass, especially being on that dreadful bus for 20 hours straight! We made it to Sheffield and played probably the best show on the tour!

London was awesome and it was amazing to actually be there and playing at the same time. Adam and I went to Camden to do some shopping and it was so bloody cold we looked like Rudolph the Red Nose Reindeer. The London show was off the hook and it felt so good to be on the road.

That first year in the band was amazing! We were working all the time. We played a sold out show at the Key Club that March and shot a video for the *"Rips the Covers Off"* album. My tech hadn't done a line check and the battery in my Wah Pedal died and was turned on which cut my signal completely out. I stood there like a jackass for half of *"Over the Edge"* with no guitar signal. I wanted to crawl in a hole! Very Spinal Tap.

Steve Riley:
We did a show at the Key Club in Hollywood not long after Stacey joined. It was set up to for us to shoot 2 videos and to shoot the entire show for a future DVD. We went on in front of a packed house with the intro tape blasting out. As soon as the intro stopped and we were to start, Stace went hit his first chord and there was nothing! After figuring out what the problem was, we went on to do a great show. But we saw something in Stace that night. He could have had a shitty night and let something like that, shooting a video in front of a packed house and your rig goes down, but instead got his shit together and carried on and had a great show. That's what it takes to survive in this business. I know both Phil and I hope that Stace hangs with us for a while.

That summer we toured with Dokken. I became good friends with everyone in that band and had a blast. It would be the first time I stepped on an American tour bus in 10 years. I loved the bus. I slept on that thing better than I did in my own bed. We had this killer driver named Ed. He was this old Harley guy with a long white beard and one of the sweetest men I have ever met. Ed was like the grandfather I never had. The tour was doing well; every show we played was packed and full of pretty girls. I became close with Mick Brown, Dokken's drummer on that tour. Mick was friggin hilarious. He's the Rodney Dangerfield of rock. Mick always had me in stitches. We would play *Grand Prix Racer* or something on XBOX on Dokken's bus while Mick played bartender and made the most awesome white russians. Mick would do the funniest things at sound check. Before Steve would come into the venue, Mick would get on Riley's drums and start playing a beat while singing gravely into the mic going "Stevorino, hanging upside down in the back lounge,

Stevorino where you at? Stevorino, come out come out, hanging with Dokken, Stevorino!"

Mick was always the life of the party and we had the same stupid sense of humor and would always break into some old *Saturday Night Live* or *SCTV* skits. We were playing in Albuquerque and Mick had this party in his suite at the hotel. He was drinking Jim Beam and Coke and couldn't find a glass, so he just filled up the coffee pot with ice and made his drink. We had a night off in Minneapolis; a lot of us went to the Hard Rock Café for some drinks and food. Mick started to buy everyone in the bar drinks. Damn, he must have spent a fortune that night. While the Ramada shuttle was taking us back the hotel, there was this elderly gentleman riding his bicycle along the street. As the shuttle drove past him, Mick rolled down the widow and screams out "Wild Mick Brown in town staying at the Ramada room 112!"

Now it wouldn't be a tour without some kind of drama, right! We banked off the tour to do three or four shows on our own. This promoter guy was doing all of them. They were in upstate NY and 1 show was just outside of Toronto. That son of a bitch stiffed us on all four shows and we lost a fuckin ton of money that week. When something like that happens on a major tour with a crew, bus and a driver it really screws your budget. I think we actually had to forfeit our salaries that week so we could stay on the road. It was like this black cloud had settled over the bus for the next few days. Everyone was pissed and really upset at the same time.

That tour also saw some drama in the Dokken camp. We were

in Allentown, Pennsylvania and Mick's drum tech and Dokken's lighting guy got into it after the concert. The drum tech took one of the floor tom stands and embedded it in this poor guys head. He's really lucky he didn't kill him. The cops came and hauled Mick's tech off to jail. That poor lighting guy showed up the next day with the nastiest gash right smack down the middle of his forehead. There was a ton of other shit that happened on that tour. We were in Oklahoma City and Dokken's tour manager was walking

Adam and I—Dokken Tour '04

down the street by the venue. This chick came up to him and asked him if he wanted a blow job. He jokingly replied "Hell Ya!" Little did he know it was a sting operation. Five cop cars swarmed in and off he went to jail. Sounds like entrapment to me. Don had to bail him out of jail later that night. Dokken had the worst luck with buses that tour. Every bus they had, the air conditioning would take a shit. They must have gone through six or seven buses.

When we were playing in North Dakota at "Rockin the Hills" a power surge hit the stage and blew up one of my amp heads. Three or four days later we were in New York City. I decided to take my head to this amp repair shop in Manhattan. I was with Ed our bus driver and Pizon our tour manager, who was from Memphis and talked like Boomhauer of "*King of the Hill*". The guy at the amp shop was an asshole and we decided to take a cab back to the bus. Pizon, funny enough had been to New York several times but never in the city. The cab driver was driving like a fuckin lunatic! Next thing we know here comes this NYPD cruiser hauling ass with his lights on from the opposite direction and this cabbie decides to try and dodge him! I swear I saw my entire life flash before my eyes. This cop car came within millimeters of demolishing us. When the cab dropped us off at the bus we said "Thanks for almost killing us asshole!" All of us were really shaken up and we all headed onto the bus and went straight for a bottle of Tequila and downed a shot. I think Pizon was most shaken up cause it was his first "real NYC cab ride."

    We did some great festivals that summer. It was the first time I played in front of a 10,000 plus crowd. The Z-92 radio festival in Omaha was the best one, 15,000 screaming rabid rock fans. It was L.A. Guns, Warrant, Ratt, Tesla, Dokken, Slaughter and Firehouse. That day was a blast and I remember Mick and me tearing around the backstage concert grounds in a golf cart that of course was manned by Mick full throttle. We almost took out the catering tent and also hit a huge hole which practically launched me out of the cart all the while Mick is laughing like a deranged maniac.

Z-92 Radio Festival – Omaha, Nebraska—
Dokken Tour '04

Before this particular festival, we were in Las Vegas and the next morning, we had to fly to Omaha but had the night off there. Steve was in rare form that night and started to party with Dokken's road crew after we played the House of Blues. I remember going into the back lounge of the bus and Steve was raising hell! Steve hardly ever partied, but when he did he was a riot! Afterwards he went out to the Hard Rock and apparently was doing buttery nipple shots. Needless to say, Steve was totally hung over the next day. He was lying on the floor of the airport while we waited for the plane. As we flew to Omaha, Riley spent most of the flight puking in the bathroom. I think he realized later that mixing red wine with buttery nipple shots may not have been a good idea. At the end of that tour I felt like it was the last day of camp. I was really bummed as we were packing up all are stuff and getting everything off the bus. We had so many cases of beer leftover we could have started our own brewery. I think Adam took ten cases home with him! I was like "Dude what are you going to do with all that beer!"

"Drink it!" he said.

At the end of August we flew into Utah to play an outdoor show in Ogden with Slaughter and Firehouse. My sister was now living in Salt Lake City. She and DJ were bringing themselves and the kids to the concert. It would be the first time my sister had seen me play since that first Blind Desire show back in '87! It was also my nephew and niece's first rock concert. Clancy was having a blast and I guess was about 9 at the time. He had a drum stick from Steve and managed to get it signed by all the other band members in Slaughter and Firehouse on his own. Ah, a chip off the old block.

That fall we went to Canada and flew into Vancouver and picked up this absolutely beautiful tour bus. We toured all the way across Canada to Toronto. It took about two hours to get through customs. Shit there must have been a thousand people in line. Tommy Chong was on our flight and we had spoken to him for a while at LAX. He said the funniest thing before we boarded the plane "Maybe I'll stick with you guys going through customs so it will take some of the heat off of me." Tommy had recently been busted for selling Bongs or something like that. It was of course raining in Vancouver, but it was great to be there. I hadn't been to Vancouver since '86. It's one of the most beautiful cities in the world. We played that night to a packed house. That tour took us through Abbotsford, B.C, Prince George, B.C., Grand Prairie, Alberta, Edmonton, Alberta, Calgary, Alberta, Saskatoon, Saskatchewan, Winnipeg, Manitoba, Thunder Bay, Ontario, Orville, Ontario and Toronto, Ontario. For the most part it was pretty good. The second or third show was in Prince George, B.C. It was way north of Vancouver and the ten hour drive up there was so scenic! I just stared out the widow for hours while I laid down in the back lounge of the bus. Anyways, there was this Mom who brought her five daughters to see us the next night. The Mom had an original L.A. Guns tour shirt from '89 and was waving it around. This guy came up and grabbed it and the Mom and daughters descended on this guy like a pack of hungry piranhas. They had him pinned against the P.A. speakers and gave him a beat down! I remember the show in Winnipeg being off the hook! They were crowd surfing and the roar of the crowd was deafening. It was a trip to be in Calgary after all those years. That night was very strange. We had the bus parked on the street behind the venue. After the show we were chilling on the bus and these drunken idiots across the street started to fuck with us. They kept yelling at us "Go back to Texas!" At one point, this fool took his pants down and started to rub his ass on the windshield of the bus. We wanted to kick this idiot's ass, but that would've ended up with the police coming and one of us going to jail for sure. Adam said "I've got a better idea." Rob the bus driver had purchased this kick ass paintball gun while we were in Winnipeg. Adam grabbed the gun and took this marksman position in the front lounge while we cracked one of the windows open and turned off all the lights. When Rob the driver got back to the bus, Adam lit that fool up like the 4th of July and we speed off!

Halfway through the tour Steve's dad fell very ill. Poor Steve had to fly to Florida after the Winnipeg show and meet up with us on a day off in Toronto. Adam actually played drums for the Thunder Bay show and we used State of Shock's (the band that was touring with us) guitarist to play bass. Speaking of State of Shock, they were a young, new band from Canada that had just gotten signed to EMI. These guys were a riot and their bassist Ally was the cutest, toughest, kick ass chick I had ever met. They were always on our bus partying. Ally would say to her band mates "If you fuckers bring any sluts to my room and use my bed I'll kick you in the NUTS!"

Jessie from State of Shock and I on our bus
—Canadian Tour '04

Jesse the guitar player was a riot. When we were in Prince George he picked up this chick and went back to her place. I guess she wouldn't put out so he left. However he didn't have any money on him and no way back to the hotel. He decided to go into this chick's garage and steal her kid's tricycle and peddle it all the way back to the hotel. I guess she had heard him in her garage and later called the cops. I can only imagine the scene of this guy with blonde and black hair peddling furiously down the road on this tricycle. The cops must have been laughing their asses off. I guess they let him go.

When we played Toronto my parents brought out some of their friends. They came a little early to hang out. My parents actually brought their friend Audrey Richardson who was 80 to the show! I think she was the most thrilled when she came on the bus. It was a very proud moment when they all came on the bus! I really felt like I had finally accomplished something. Four of my high school buddies came to the Toronto show and it was amazing to see these guys after 15 years!

I had decided to stay three extra days in Toronto so I could catch up with my parents and some friends. It had been years since I had been home. That last night we had stayed at the Travelodge and had one last blowout on the bus. My old band mate Bruce from Fraidy Katt had come out that night and I had not seen him since '92! When I woke up in the morning the bus was gone and Steve, Adam and Phil had already split. It was a weird feeling kind of like my familiar world had just vanished. My dad came and picked me up and we headed back to their condo. It was really strange being back in Toronto. That night I hooked up with Bruce and met him downtown. It was surreal to ride the subway downtown, something I hadn't done in almost 13 years. Over the next few days I just took it easy and caught up with old friends. That Sunday I went with my parents to my old church. People were tripping out when they saw me. I hadn't been to my church in almost 15 years. During the service, this huge wave of emotion came over me. I guess it was God speaking to me or something, but it was very powerful. I think too, I had basically grown up in that church.

In October, we went back to Europe again and went to Greece and Turkey for the first time. The first two days were hellacious. We flew from L.A. to London, spent the night in London. Of course the English road crew dragged me to the hotel bar, (well not really) and started to pound beers .One thing about the English, they can sure put 'em away. The next morning we had to fly from London to Istanbul, Turkey and then fly to Ankara and friggin play that night! By the time we got to Ankara we were fried. It was so weird in Ankara; I swear we might as well have been in Cairo. So we go straight to the venue, and the promoter really didn't have his shit together because the gear was kind of a joke. I think the cymbals were held together with bottle caps and they had these cheap solid state Marshalls. So we blast into *"No Mercy"* and one of those cheap heads blows. My tech plugs me into the other head and we start *"Sex Action."* Pooofffff there goes the second head.

Now there is one other amp and Phil is playing through that one. So there I am completely jet lagged and ampless standing there screaming at the promoter! I was pissed and unplugged my guitar and walked off stage. The guys finished "Sex Action" and Chris my tech grabbed the other Marshall. Now this other head was one of those old 100 watt Marshall Plexi heads that if you turn up past two you're changing people's chromosomes. I was so loud that our soundman took me out of the mix completely. Leaving Ankara felt good and they had picked us up in one of those big shuttle vans. We had a long eight hour drive and I remember looking at the driver from time to time as he was starting to nod off. We got to Istanbul and had the night off. That concert the next night was one of the most insane shows I have ever played. It's like they had never seen a rock band from the U.S. before. We had to walk through the crowd to get to the stage and I though they were going to rip us to pieces! The place went nuts and I remember about 500 people jumping up and down as the stage started to rock like a boat on a choppy ocean.

Turkey is a strange place and they have all these mosques every where. At 5:45 am the "Call to Prayer" goes off and is broadcast very loud all over the city, nothing like hearing that in your hotel room bright and early.

The next morning we headed to the airport in a convoy of these tiny cabs. The promoter had left us to fend for ourselves. All of these cabs were hauling ass to the airport. It looked like a scene out of the "*Italian Job*". We made our flight from Istanbul to

Athens. We then had to change planes and fly into Thessaloniki. We got on this ancient Olympus jet. There was a really bad rain storm flying into Thessaloniki and we hit the most insane turbulence I had ever experienced. I really thought "this is it, we're gonna die!" I even recall a wind sheer hitting us and it felt like a giant hand slapped the plane. My hands were practically soaked with blood from gripping the seatbelt so tight. That night we played a beautiful theater and the place went nuts. Greece was my new favorite place. We had the next 2 days off. The promoters there were amazing and really took care of us. Everybody went to T.G.I. Fridays and it was a beautiful sunny day and we were just blocks from the Aegean Sea. I had never seen so many beautiful, women in one place at one time. It was like that island that Wonder Woman came from. I remember sitting on my balcony of my hotel at night watching the street traffic while smoking a cigarette going "Thank you God!" The next night we flew into Madrid and picked up this really nice single decker bus. The rest of that tour took us through Spain, Switzerland, Italy, and the U.K. We had taken this young soundman with us. I think his name was Will. He looked like Harry Potter. This dude would fuckin drink like no man I'd ever seen! He would get so fucked up that he started to have that Frankenstein look going on. One night on the bus he thought the garbage can was the toilet and shit in it and all over him self. I remember my tech Chris Tudor-Jones grabbing him by the neck and throwing him off the bus then hosing him down. I think Will shit himself again a few nights later.

We couldn't believe this kid pulled the same routine two nights later. I'm pretty sure we clipped his alcohol consumption for the rest of the tour.

Now, one thing about Europe is that the food is either really good, horrible or mysterious. The night we played in Barcelona, Spain the promoter took us to this mediocre restaurant for dinner. When we walked in they had all these pictures of the meals served and by one look I knew we were in for a shit meal. After thumbing through the menu I noticed they had calamari. Adam and I had it the night before in Madrid and it was awesome. So I figured I would play it safe and order just that. When my meal was brought out to me I was horrified. This didn't look like any Calamari I had in the past. Basically they brought me out an entire squid: eyeballs, tentacles and all. The band and crew just stared at my plate and me. I was starving and said "Fuck it!" I dove in with my knife and fork. It was like cutting into a Dunlop tennis ball. It actually tasted pretty good. I gained new respect from the band that night. However they were all laughing and fucking with me. Shit, even the waiter brought me a roll of toilet paper.

I got to spend my 36th birthday in London. We played that night in Islington which was a lot different than Camden, nevertheless the show was sold out and we slayed London one more time. I was living out my dream finally and I soaked every minute of it up.

This club had an after party for us and had rented out the top floor for us. We had a ton of fun that night and Steve and I were having blast holding court! I remember looking over at Tudor-

Jones at one point and he had like 13 beers in his hand. I thought to myself "I hope those aren't all for him?" then again he was an Englishman.

Thessaloniki Greece---L.A. Guns European Tour '04

We finished the rest of the year off with a show in Long Beach with our good buddies Dokken. Towards the last part of that year my marriage was starting to hit the bricks. I was so wrapped up in my new found fame that I had single handedly pushed my wife away. It came to a head that night in Long Beach and on the way home Lisa and I had this massive fight. She told me that was it and she was moving back to Florida. I agreed to take her back to Florida and we drove her car all the way back there. After Christmas she packed all of her stuff into her car and off we went to spend four and half days driving across America again.

I flew back to L.A. and walked into my apartment and felt really weird. Wow, Lisa was really gone. It really took a lot of time to get used to her not being there. Not only that, but my bills just doubled. I won't lie. I really started to feel the crunch somewhat financially being own my own without that second income.

STACEY GET YOUR GUN

Chapter 9

The winter and spring of 2005 we started doing a lot of fly-ins. Basically what this is, is that you would fly into let's say Cleveland and play three or four shows in that area, i.e: Cleveland, Toledo, Dayton and Cincinnati and then fly back to L.A. We had this guy working for us who Adam had known in high school back in Louisiana. Holman was a good worker but a time bomb waiting to blow.

We had a show to do in New York City in March. Before the Manhattan show, we had the night off and Lee was staying in Manhattan with these three girls from Florida. Holman and I decide to take one of the vans into the city from Jersey where we were staying. We had fun that night and hit about three or four hotspots. Of course Holman got hammered and spent like 300 bucks at the bar. I had been drinking too, thinking that he was going to drive home. By the end of the night I practically had to carry him back to the car and I had no idea how to get back to the hotel in Jersey. I had had a few drinks as well and never drove if I had been drinking. I swear a guardian angel guided me out of Manhattan, through the Lincoln tunnel and back to the hotel.

The weather was horrible in New York and I've never seen rain like that in my life. It was a bitch of a day because the rain made the traffic hell and we had to go back and forth from Jersey twice that day. Driving in New York City is a feat in itself. I remember we told Steve to take a right onto this street. Little did we know we would be turning onto a one way street the wrong way. We saw tons of car lights bearing down on us as we all screamed "One Way, One Way!!" Steve adopted the nickname "Right Here Riley" after that. That night we played a packed show at the Continental in the Village. I was surprised anybody was out considering the typhoon that was going on outside. On the way back to Jersey we got lost and took the wrong tunnel and ended up going the opposite way. Then we had to turn around then got lost in Manhattan. Thankfully this hooker gave us directions to the Lincoln Tunnel. I had to piss so bad that it was coming out my eyeballs. I had been holding it in for like 45 minutes. I swear, I must have pissed for five minutes straight in the parking lot of the Howard Johnson as the rain and wind pelted me.

Phil Lewis - L.A.Guns Lead Vocalist:
The first time I met Stacey he came over to play some slide guitar on a couple of songs, It didn't take too long for me to realize he was the "real deal," Of course he played the guitar like a demon and his whole look and style were totally authentic, But the thing that I liked most, was his personality and charm. Almost five years later and many thousand of miles he has continued to render me in sometimes almost painful sessions of uncontrollable laughter on our many adventures. Stacey loves being on the road and the road loves him. He is talented, bright and at times very saucy and has once again impressed me with a new undiscovered talent for story writing.

That May, we entered the studio once again with Andy Johns to record "*Tales from the Strip*". We had worked many months on writing and we felt we really needed to step up to the plate and deliver an album that would be stellar. It was the first original L.A. Guns record without Tracii. It was awesome to be working with Andy again. He would complement me quite a bit while I was laying down my guitar tracks. I just wanted to hug the guy! I think it was the biggest pat on the back that I needed. I savored every second of making that record. I really could tell we were making an amazing record. When Phil started laying down his vocals, we were all levitating on how good these songs sounded.

Andy and Phil had quite the banter between those two. They were either joking and laughing with each other or screaming and telling each other off. There were a few times I had to chase Andy down the street from leaving. I really thought we had made an amazing record and judging by the reviews we got, we did just that! I thought everyone in the band had really stepped up and brought everything they had to the plate. Songs like "*Skin,*" "*Electric Neon Sunset,*" "*Shame,*" "*Vampire,*" and "*It Don't Mean Nothing*" really stood out.

Sleaze Roxx Magazine Review:

I looked forward to picking this CD up with such anticipation, I actually bought one on Amazon on August 12. But, I just couldn't wait those few extra days and ended up buying it at the store as well to hear it a second early. Do I regret it? Not at all!

What can I possibly say about this record other than the standard, "It rocks, dude?" Quite frankly, that sums it up. But, let me get into more detail about what is so great about this record.

First, every song is at least good. Some are better than others but there isn't a stinker on here that will require you to get up and change tracks because your ears are bleeding.

The best songs off the record, or at least the ones that jump out at me at this moment after having listened to it all the way through 3 times, are the opening track of "It Don't Mean Nothing," "Electric Neon Sunset," "Gypsy Soul," Skin," and "(Can't Give You) Anything But Love." But, no song is "bad." As a matter of fact, I chose those songs because they are the ones that I most clearly remember. Any song could really be my favorite off the record.

Some are concerned about the lack of Tracii Guns on this record. I say, "Tracii who?" Tracii's off trying to be modern and performing piss poor punk music in South America somewhere. Tracii's a great guitarist, don't get me wrong. But, as much as I pick on Steven Tyler for being vocally shot, Tracii Guns is creatively shot and it's a real shame. But Stacey Blades fits the bill nicely and damn does he play a mean guitar.

Yes, all you ska and punk fans, this record has guitar solos! Guitar solos are instrumental solos performed by good musicians that add to the songs. I think the lack of guitar solos in the modern rock scene is directly related to the lack of talented guitarists. Stacey's got all the talent in the world!

Is it better than *Waking The Dead*? I can't say yes and I can't say no. It's simply different. *Waking The Dead* was a slightly more modern record and, at times, a slightly heavier one.

Tales From The Strip is still heavy but sounds more like what most of us remember L.A. Guns as being. I love *Waking The Dead* and also love *Tales From The Strip*. How neither of these records were blockbuster hits is beyond me. Or, maybe they're just too good and piss poor bands like Jimmy Eat World would be exposed as piss poor in comparison.

The last song on the disc is "(Can't Give You) Anything But Love." It's clear to me that a lot of love went into this album. And, they did give us something better than love. They gave us a fantastic album that you all should buy. They gave me and all of us, *Tales From The Strip*!

**Recording Tales From the Strip---
Me and Andy Johns-- May '05**

That summer we went out on the *"American Metal Blast Tour"* with WASP, Stephen Pearcy, and Metal Church. We did like 50 shows in 58 days.

Once again we were able to get a bus with a shower on it and get good ole Ed to drive for us. We knew we were in good hands. The crew however was a different story. We were fried halfway through and Holman our tour manager turned into this complete disheveled lunatic. I swear the guy was bi-polar but I think it may have been a chemical reaction to beer and pot. One night in Sayreville, New Jersey he snapped. While my guitar tech was putting my Les Paul away, Mr. Bi- Polar shoved Darren into a road case and shaved an inch long gash off the neck of my guitar. When I found this out I flipped! I confronted him and he snapped. He got all in my face and threw me into a wall. I saw red and jumped on him and it took 2 people to pull me off of him. I was ready to kill that S.O.B. Word traveled quickly and the entire security staff from the venue wanted to take him into the woods! So the bus leaves to go to the hotel and this maniac is still ranting. We almost stopped a few times and kicked him off the bus. We got to the hotel and everybody headed inside. I was the only one who didn't have a room and was stuck on the bus with this psycho! I thought the guy would've calmed down by now but he was about to crank it up a notch. He started to scream and bang his fist against the counters of the galley in the front lounge of the bus. He was screaming so hard that he was foaming at the mouth. It was like watching a train wreck. I had never seen a human being act like this in my life. I didn't know whether to laugh or run for cover. Needless to say we sacked his ass the next day.

That WASP Tour saw us all crumble. Adam and Phil were numbing themselves on a daily basis with tons of pills. There were so many times that I would wake up and climb out of my bunk and pray for these guys not to be dead. I was coping in weird ways as well. I started making these drinks which I called Zombie Juice. You take a big plastic cup, fill it with ice and put half Red Bull and half a Corona in it with a slice of lime. I called it Zombie Juice because it numbed your brain but kept your body awake. Too many of these things would tweak you out, that you might as well have been snorting blow! I found out I couldn't go on stage without downing at least 2 or 3 of these. Of course I would end up drinking these all the way into the wee hours of the morning and be completely tweaked out drunk curled up in a corner somewhere, then have to take a Xanax to come down. For some reason, that tour was just so stressful and draining.

Adam Hamilton:
The summer the band got to tour with Wasp was one not soon forgotten. Or was it.... I think we all did so much damage to ourselves on that tour that I personally can't remember a lot of it. I do know that we were super excited to get the tour. Steve having been in Wasp, made the whole thing even more interesting. How was Blackie going to treat us? Well, we figured if he harbored any animosity toward Steve, we probably would not have gotten on the tour. It would be interesting none the less.
We loved Stephen Pearcy whom the band had known for years and we really got to like after a few fly in shows with him in the years before. We met Mike Duda at the Cinderella show about a month before the tour began. I wasn't too sure what to make of him at our first encounter. He seemed very drunk and slightly frightening. Little did I know that he would become like a big brother to me and look out for us out there that summer. The tour began with a bang and everyone got along brilliantly. All three bands appreciated and

respected what each did and we collectively screamed "game on!" Although as great as the Wasp guys were, their dark leader was less than warm and cordial. It may sound clichéd to say but, "it was a party every night" and then some. I have always admired how some people can party for days and then just have some kind of restraint and know when not to... More on that later... The three tour buses parked in a row was always and exciting sight to see when we finally came to and rolled out of our booze and drug induced comas. Not to incriminate anyone else, I will only speak for myself on the latter. We would finally come to in some new town and throw on a pair of filthy jeans and the first pair of sunglasses handy. Our bus was called "The Rainbow" and The Pearcy guys bus was "the Viper Room". Very appropriately named I think. Parked side by side you could attend one of the two possible after parties and when it was time for a change of venue all one had to do was walk over to the next bus and join in the all night party already in effect. We would crank the music and drink and drug ourselves into comas every night. I repeat, every night.

As much fun as we were having, we were disappointed in some of the turnouts in certain cities. Even having a show cancelled the day of the show in Texas. We just drank and partied more. We did have a hard time with that one. Come on! "Blind in Texas"! That was one of their best markets!! Depressing! We drank and partied more. As the tour wound down we lost a few crew members along the way. So much drugging and drinking were taking its toll on us for sure. It was a really hard summer. It had started out great and was starting to become a real drag! We drank and partied more. This time it was to forget how bad of a tour it was becoming. I know that I had landed in the full throws of a serious alcohol and drug problem by the time we returned at the end of summer. All in all, it was like the Charles Dickens novel "A Tale of Two Cities," it begins, "It was the best of times, it was the worst of times." We really had refined the art of living the life of a pirate for sure. I think Phil and I kind of took it to the next level. Steve and Stacey seemed to know when to say when. I will never forget Stacey saying to me" there were days when I wasn't sure if you and Phil were gonna crawl out of your bunks alive" That really stuck with me. After the tour I knew I had to make some changes because I am not sure how many more summers like that I had in me.

This asshole in Fargo had hosed us for a couple grand. Oh yeah I almost got arrested that night for walking outside with a beer. I guess "Barney Fife" saw me and was grilling me saying he was going to take me to jail, pleeeaazzze! I wanted to slug that cop so bad but of course I just kept my mouth shut. A week later we were in New Orleans and I met my first stalker. If you've never had anybody do this to you, it is very unsettling to say the least. I was chilling on the bus before sound check and one of Stephen Pearcy's crew guys comes on the bus and asks me if I would take a few pictures with this girl. I said "Yeah I'll be right out." I met this tall Japanese girl and took a few pictures with her and then she gave me a bunch of gifts and a card. I thought it was endearing and it was a little awkward because her English wasn't all that good. I came back on the bus and opened up the card. The card basically said "My name is so and so and I'm a big fan of yours. I'm very lonely and don't know that many people in L.A. and really love you." She also included her phone number in it. I gave the card to Adam to read and asked him what he thought. Adam read the card and looked at me strangely and said "Dude that's kind of creepy" I was like "Dude you took the words right out of my mouth." She showed up again a week later in Vegas. After the show we went and did the meet and greet like we always did and this weirdo starts chasing me out of the venue and into the Casino. She handed me another gift and card, which basically said the same thing. I knew right then and there that this girl was going to be a problem.

In mid August WASP was going over to Europe for a few festivals. We had I think five shows on our own before the second leg of the tour started. Of course these shows started looking very shady. We had the day off in Vegas and Steve decided to pull the plug and pull the wagon back home. Everyone in a way was relieved but I think we still wanted to work. It felt like that black cloud had settled over the bus again. We drove back to L.A. and the bus dropped us off in front of my place. We pulled all our shit off the bus and I remember just sitting in my apartment with all my crap just staring at the wall. My neighbor Darren came over with a glass of wine and just kept cracking up because I was so completely out of it and could barely form a sentence.

Two days later Steve called and said that the shows we were supposed to do in Colorado were on! The promoter stepped up and paid for our flights. So off we go again. The show in Aurora was great and the next day we drove to this place near Aspen. It was an absolute ridiculous gig. I guess this ex-stripper who owned this bar had dished all this money out for us to play there. The place didn't even have a stage. By show time everyone in the club was wasted and there was this one guy who was in charge of security trying to hold all these drunken fuckers back. I just wanted the show to be done and I kept yelling at this club owner (the ex- stripper) to do something about it! Next thing I know I got completely doused with a full plastic cup of Jack and Coke. We made it through the show and it was miserable. While we were waiting for some food after the show the club owner said "Hey guys instead of steak sandwiches do you want some cocaine!" We headed back to L.A. and decided that we needed to finish the second leg of the tour. We had decided originally not to, but since our new album had just come out we felt it was a good idea to be back on the road. Funny enough we were able to get the same bus again and Ed driving it. We dead headed two days to Texas and finished up the last two weeks of the tour.

Three weeks after the summer tour we left for another European tour. We were fried and that tour was hell. We flew into Milan, Italy to start the tour. We thought we would try and cut some corners to make more money on the tour and boy did that come back to bite us in the ass! We were going to do ground transportation and flights for the first two weeks and then pick up a bus when we got to the U.K. We decided to take Darren who guitar tech'd for us on the WASP tour. This guy fell to pieces and I mean pieces on this tour. We should have let him go after the summer. He shows up to the airport with huge black eyeliner on wearing a track suit. He misplaced his passport within 5 minutes. Some TSA guy comes up to us and says "Does this belong to your group." Phil says, "Yeah I'll take that." We then decided to have some fun with Darren. "Okay everybody get your passports out!" We watched Darren completely scramble as his face started to turn white. "Looking for this?" Darren put us all through the ringer. The guy had so many meltdowns, misplaced gear and had the worst attitude. When we were in Switzerland he misplaced Riley's cymbals. We were furious and Darren thought he had lost them. He was convinced that we were going to cash his plane ticket in to cover the cost of Steve's cymbals. We still laugh about this to this day. Darren had this funny southern accent even though he was from Maryland. When he thought he was in deep for $1500 for the cymbals, a tear rolled down his eye as he blurted out in this shaky southern drawl "Why does this shit only happen to me man, now I got to figure out how I'm getting back to the States!"

Like true L.A. Guns style we blew it out the first night in Milan. The next day we all had to cram our hung over asses into this van and drive to the next gig. The next night we were in Rome and I had already started to get sick with the flu, which in turn got everyone else sick. Those guys wanted to kick my ass! We had to wake up at the crack of dawn and fly from Rome to Munich. When we were at the airport in Rome the airline really fucked us with the weight charges on our merchandise. I remember Steve walking back to us with this look of shock while shaking his head. "I just had to pay the airline 2600 bucks in overweight baggage charges," he said. It really didn't register at first and then it sunk in, Oh shit! Well here comes that black cloud again. We played in Munich that night and everyone was really starting to get sick and giving me the death eye for giving them the flu! Thank God we had the next day off. I laid in my bed all day in my hotel room and watched German T.V. Nothing like watching a James Bond movie with German overdubs. We flew to Thessaloniki the next day. As we were walking out of the airport this guy comes up to us and flashes his badge and says, "You, you, you and you come with me." They pulled us into this room and went through all our shit. Those assholes went through everything, even hand lotion and cotton swabs. They were putting everything through this machine to see if drug residue would show up. I remember the guy saying that one of my Q-Tips had cocaine residue on it. I told the guy "Well you better get another machine because that's an out and out lie!" These turds let us go and they looked disappointed that they came up empty handed. Greece was great as usual. We only had the one show there and it was a 24 hour Shangri-la. We sat out in the sun that afternoon and ate steak, dipped French bread in olive oil and sipped on white wine. We savored every second of it because by the crack of dawn we knew we would be up and running again. By the time we hit London, Steve was spitting up blood. I think he had gotten a bronchiole infection and was losing it quickly. The poor guy was miserable. Darren once again to the rescue had lost Steve's Ludwig drum head and Steve lost it. The whole tour had been a kick in the nuts, not only for him but for the rest of us as well. I remember Steve talking to himself as we walked through Camden to go to sound check. The London show as usual was off the hook and the next day, we were getting on this kick ass double decker tour bus. The rest of the tour was pretty good, we had gone to Ireland for the first time and it was really cool being in Belfast. They went nuts for us that night and I think a few chicks tackled Phil while we were doing the meet and greet.

Tour Bus---England, L.A. Guns
European Tour —Fall '05

We finished the tour in Nottingham and drove back to London on the bus as they dropped us off at Heathrow. Phil had decided to stay in London for a few days and that flight back to L.A. couldn't have been longer!

After that tour we were all in our own private little hells. Adam and Phil were getting addicted to pills, Steve had recently lost his father and I had fucked up my marriage and was separated. We took the rest of the year off and boy did we need it!

I decided to go to Florida and see Lisa, while I soaked up some sun and chilled on the beach. Lisa was staying with her parents and lived about two minutes from Treasure Island Beach in St. Petersburg. It felt good to be in Florida for a change and it was nice to relax after being completely burnt from the summer and fall tour.

One afternoon while Lisa and I were shopping, we were walking back to the car and I hear this girl say "Stacey?" I turned around and it was Christine! I was kind of surprised to see her. I walked over to her car and she was with her stripper mom. Her mom was actually really cool and she says to me "I just started to work over at so and so place." All I could think was "Shit, this woman is still dancing?" I introduced Chris and her mom to Lisa. Of course I didn't mention to Chris that we were separated. This was my chance to really rub it in to this girl. I still hadn't forgotten about the utter hell she put me through. She said, "How the hell are you!" Of course I replied, "I'M GREAT, Yep living in L.A., been playing in L.A. Guns for the last couple of years and touring the world." She then told me that she had gotten divorced from that loser she had married. (The guy she dumped me for). She also ended up having a kid with this guy and eluded that she was living back with her mom. We made some small chit chat and I remember her mom saying "Chris why don't you take a picture with him, he's a star now." I'm sure as we left, Chris got on the phone and called Jamie and told her "Guess who I just ran into!" While Lisa and I were walking back to the car, I could hear the sound of *South Park's* Eric Cartman going "Revenge is so very, very sweet" in my head.

While I was in Florida that week, it just so happens that the *VH1 Metal Mania Stripped* tour featuring Don Dokken, Stephen Pearcy, Firehouse, Jani Lane and Kip Winger was playing in Clearwater. My old tech Kevin who was working on that tour hooked us up with passes. The show was pretty cool and it was great to catch up with Stephen, Don, the Firehouse guys and Frankie Wilsex from Stephen Pearcy's band.

As I was watching the show backstage I noticed my friend Tracy who used to dance at Diamond Dolls. I hadn't seen her in like ten years! It was great to catch up with her and we all went to the tour bus and had drinks with everybody. Later that night Tracy and her friend took me, Lisa, Frankie and Reb Beech to some stupid dance club. Of course they VIP'D us. Florida is a very small circle. The manager at that club was the old DJ at Diamond Dolls, (I told you I spent a lot of time there). We split that place and went back to the bus for a few more drinks. Anytime I was on a bus I immediately reverted to road life. A few nights later we hooked up with Tracy and went to some stupid beach bar called the Daiquiri Deck and met up with some of her friends who I hadn't seen in years. We quickly got bored and went to the Dollhouse and then The Hard Rock Casino. Next thing we know it's like four in the morning. You can pretty much hit the best bars in Tampa, Clearwater and St. Pete in one night. The next day was Thanksgiving and Lisa and I were hurting. We ate turkey and pretty much passed out at 7'oclock that night. I had to get up at five and catch a 7:45 am flight back to L.A.

Phil was having a long overdue wedding reception at the Cat Club a few days later. There were about 30 people there and we had the club to ourselves for a few hours. Phil's wife had her parents fly in from Japan. Her father gave the most endearing speech while his other daughter translated. After that there was this big commotion. Leave it up to Phil to make it interesting. There was a line of Kabuki Nuns storming in from the back of the club screaming "Stop the Wedding!!!" as they threw confetti like Rip Taylor. They came up on stage and basically roasted Phil. It was an interesting night to say the least and we went up on stage and played "Over the Edge," "Never Enough," *and* "Sex Action."

Earlier that same year, I had gotten to know this publicist and her daughter. They both liked to tell tall tales and it was so hard at times to believe anything that came out of their mouths. Anyways the publicist used to get me into all kinds of media events. That year she had gotten Jon Levin and I front row seats at the Agent

Provocateur fashion show during "Fashion Week." As Jon and I were waiting in the lobby having a drink, Cher walked 2 feet past me. Now I'm not usually star struck at all but shit, this was Cher! I had grown up watching her as a kid. I nudged Jon's shoulder and said "Dude, there's fuckin Cher!" He was like, "Yeah, so what." The show was awesome, I mean front row at a lingerie show! Across from me was Courtney Love, Carmen Electra, Kimberly Stewart, Anthony Kiedis, Rebecca De Mornay, Tara Lipinski and ten seats from me was Christina Auguilera. It felt weird being in the same room with all these famous people. To be honest I couldn't wait to leave once the show was done. It really wasn't my kind of scene and I felt like a fish out of water.

Lisa had decided to come out to L.A. for Christmas. I wanted to go to Home Depot and get a tree and really try and decorate the place up for Lisa. I got what looked like a modest tree and it was wrapped up in mesh. I lugged the tree across the parking lot and put it in the trunk of my Thunderbird. Once I got it into the apartment and cut the mesh it was like "Woooooosh." That tree must have been 12 feet wide! I was like "whoa, I'm going to be cleaning up pine needles for years." I picked Lisa up at LAX the day before Christmas and I remember it was like 88 degrees that day. Lisa and I were getting along pretty good. I guess being away from each other was working. But in spite of good times, we still had our moments here and there when we fought like cats and dogs.

A week before Christmas, Andy Johns had a Christmas party. Andy always had the best parties and barbeques. I loved going over to Andy's place and his son Evan was such a great and cool kid. Andy was always very entertaining and he could go on for hours about stories of old. I personally loved hearing him talk about Mick and Keith and Jimmy Page. Andy has this really cool room in the back of his house with all the albums he's produced framed on the wall. Andy was holding court as usual and talking in his loud boisterous English accent with a drink in one hand and a smoke dangling from his lips. During that moment, Andy's wife Annette came into the room, smiled at everybody then proceeded to move Andy's chair. Now when Andy was done with his conversation, he thought he would just sit back down, wrong! It was like slow motion. He's waiting for that comfort zone of the chair, he's waiting, waiting, BOOM!!! Andy went down like a sack of concrete blocks. Now Andy is a pretty big guy and I swear the room shook. We all saw ripples in his face as he hit the ground. We tried not to laugh but Steve, Phil and I went running out of the room pissing ourselves. It was one of the funniest things I've seen. We started wondering if Annette moved his chair on purpose. I mean, they had been married for a long time.

That New Year the band had switched agencies and we had a new manager as well. We started off the year with a show at the Whisky that we were going to film for a live DVD and also record for a live album *"Loud And Dangerous"* to be released in late spring early summer. It was a packed show and we really kicked ass that night! I noticed immediately that my Japanese stalker was right in front of me. I noticed that she was filming the show with her camera, but wasn't filming the band just me. It really started to creep me out. Later that night once the show was over I ventured downstairs and of course there she was holding a big paper bag. She came up to me and said "This is for you!" She had gotten me this velvet embroidered jacket that must have been from Japan and a box of Godiva chocolates with of course another stupid card in it. I didn't say much and thanked her as I walked away. I got upstairs and opened the card which read something like "please be my Valentine, and I really must have you." I didn't know whether to laugh or shake my head.

Two weeks later Phil and I were at the NAMM Music Convention in Anaheim. If you've never been there, it's basically a big schmooze fest with all the music manufacturers, i.e. guitars, amps, string companies, pianos and keyboards, you get the idea. It's a complete madhouse and a very draining day. Phil and I went over to the Crate Amplifier booth. Earlier that year we had scored a really good endorsement with those guys. They had actually printed up my endorsement shot I did for them for the amps and had blown it up really big. It was a great stroke to my ego and I felt really appreciated for a change. Anyways shortly after we left the Crate booth, Phil and I were talking to a few people and I feel this tap on my shoulder and turn around and it's my stalker! Holy Shit, I thought how on earth did this weirdo find me here! I was convinced that this girl was definitely following me now. I looked at Phil with this panicked look on my face and he knew to pull me away quickly. Overall it was a fun day and we scored a B.C. Rich endorsement. A few weeks later there was this play called "Rock of Ages" that we got invited to.

It was the premiere night in L.A. and it was a star studded event. It would be the first time I walked the "Red Carpet" with the paparazzi flashes going off. It was damn cool! That night we sat in the front and watched this musical with our buddies from Dokken, Quiet Riot, Stephen Pearcy, Jack Blades, and C.C. Deville. The play was about a small town girl moving to L.A. to make it big while she worked at this bar called "Rock of Ages." The cast included Laura Bell Bundy and Kyle Gass to name a few.

Rock of Ages Premier '06

The show was fun and afterward there was a big party. Me and the band rubbed elbows with Debra Gibson, Amber Smith, Jonathan Silverman, Fred Dryer and Perry Farrell. That winter I had become good friends with WASP bassist Mike Duda. Mike and I hung out a lot when we were both in town. We were so much alike. We had the same intense musical drive and were both adopted and had that fucked up sense about us of "Just who the hell were we?" That winter Lee had decided to move to L.A. He had sold his condo in Miami and asked if he could stay with me until he got settled. It was great having my best friend at my digs. It really took the boredom out of life when I would be off the road. With the new agency in tow, we started to work a lot! That spring we were on the road for pretty much 8 weeks straight with a few days off here and there. We were flying all the time and I think the entire staff at LAX knew us on a first name basis. Before we left to go on the road, Adam had decided to get clean and sober. He told us that he was an addict and we all kind of laughed. We were like "No your not!" but the truth of it was that he really was getting out of control with the pills. Adam did a good job at concealing his drug use. Once he poured his heart out, we were kind of shocked and realized he really was fucked up. I've got to hand it to Adam, he didn't once fall off the wagon. He stuck to his sobriety and still does to this day. It was very hard for him though, especially when we played. The rest of us still partied around him but he didn't seem phased by it. He had told me that it was miserable the first few times he had gone on stage completely sober. Towards the end of that tour Adam seemed less and less thrilled to be on the road. I can't imagine being in that situation. Adam had also been going to a therapist. I think his onion was getting peeled quickly and there were times when he confided in us that he was losing his mind!

After that spring tour, things seemed to dry up work wise. I didn't understand it. Summer was approaching and we should have been gearing up for a lot of work but we just ended up working only one week out of that whole summer! We thought something fishy was going on with our manager and agency.

Over Memorial Day Weekend, Andy John's had one of his famous barbeques. Andy kept going on and on about Roy Thomas Baker showing up. I brought Lee for extra entertainment and thought he would get a kick out of Andy. About an hour into the barbeque I see this eccentric fellow walk into Andy's dressed in gold shoes, Beatle glasses and a blue double breasted blazer with an ascot. I was like "Holy Shit, That's got to be RTB." Now he was legendary. RTB had produced Cheap Trick and all those famous Queen Albums! He was accompanied by his wife Teri, who was a fox! Adam and I shot the shit with RTB and it was cool to hear some old stories from him. I started to talk a lot with Teri and she was really cool! She told me about all those crazy parties they would have in the early 80's with Motley and whatnot. The more I talked with Teri I could swear she was flirting with me big time. Teri and I exchanged numbers and I felt it would be really cool to get to know these two better. Teri and I talked a few times on the phone and made plans for sushi but of course in L.A. rarely do plans like that ever surface. Over June, I got very bored quickly and started to climb the walls. Fortunately Lee was living in L.A. now and helped me occupy my time. I kind of fell into a depression by being at home for so many weeks. Mike Duda from WASP was kind of in the same situation and was home a bit that summer as well. Mike, Lee and I went out all the time. We started to party so much, I think out of complete boredom. Being on the road and working becomes kind of like breathing air. When you don't do it for a while or are at home for too long, you start to suffocate; well at least Mike and I felt that way.

I hated staying at home because I would just stare at the walls and still really wasn't used to the fact that Lisa and I were separated. Lee and I would do Mondays at the Key Club, Wednesdays at Jones's on Santa Monica, Thursday and Friday at the Rainbow. We were partying so much and I was really starting to get completely out of control.

Lee Markel:
As crazy as things were that summer, we would usually follow a routine but sometimes we would change the venue. One night we started at the Standard's bar on Sunset and as usual the drinks (and other things) were flowing freely. One minute I was finishing my first drink and the next minute (three hours later) I was getting my car and the valet employees were trying to stop me from driving. A lanky man in a valet vest jumped into the car and said, "You're not going anywhere bud!" I quipped, "You're in a rented vehicle with a drunken maniac and about to go on the ride of your life!" He bailed out as I was steering the SUV onto Sunset and about that time Blades is jogging towards me yelling for me to hold up and with the passenger door still open. Blades grabbed the handle, and with his body hanging out of the vehicle and his shoes sparking down the Sunset Strip pavement, he made

his way into the car. Just another Tuesday evening.

Lee had moved into this killer new apartment complex called the Palazzo. He was renting this second floor bungalow. One day in June we hung at the pool and got pretty sun burned. I went home and Lee decided to meet up with this clothes designer for cocktails at Arnie Mortons. We were later meeting that night to go see WASP play at the Key Club. My old S.M.A.C.K. bandmate Jaime met me at my place and Lee was going to come over and we were all going to head up to the Key club together. Lee calls around 9 o'clock and he's fuckin hammered. I guess the sun earlier that day had knocked Lee out and when he went to the restaurant he didn't eat anything and knocked back a ton of drinks. Earlier that year Lee had gotten this kickass red Acura NSX. Lee told me on the phone that he was jumping in the hot rod and would meet us at the club. I sternly told him NO! "Dude you are hammered and do not get in your car!" He simply replied "See ya up there Blades" and hung up. I called him back immediately and told him "Dude do not get in your car, we will come get you," he replied the same way, "See you up there Blades, I'm jumping in the Hot Rod!" and hung up on me again. Now I had partied with Lee a million times, but I could tell he was really out of it. Jamie was like "What the hell is that nut doing" I said, "Watch Jamie, that joker's going to get a DUI." Jamie and I headed up to the Key Club and chatted with a few people outside and then made our way into the venue. As soon as we walked in, Boom! There's my wonderful stalker! I was like "Oh great!" I soon ran into Lee and he had successfully made it there. He looked completely decimated. I grabbed his beer and said "That's it for you my friend". We went downstairs and ran into my buddy Jon Levin from Dokken. After a few minutes Jon started laughing and said "Lee just got bounced out of here." I started to worry about him but figured he would have the sense to call a cab and just go home. As I went to the bar to get a beer my stalker descended on me like a swarm of angry bees. She actually started video taping me getting a beer at the bar, and was totally in my face. That was it, I'd had enough! I grabbed her camera and shoved her back and told her to fuck off! You would think that would have deterred her? Hell no! Two minutes later she comes up to me again with one of those stupid cards. I told her to get the hell away and knocked the card out of her hand. Jamie and I whisked ourselves upstairs quickly. I started to have this very uneasy feeling. I mean did this chick make these cards up and then carry them around with the hopes of running into me? Or did she know exactly where I was going to be? WASP kicked ass and it was a great show. It was Mike's birthday and after the show we headed over to the Cat Club for some "after hours" festivities. The whole night I kept thinking "Boy, I hope Lee is all right." The next morning the phone woke me up and it was Lee. "Well Blades it appears I got a DUI last night and I'm walking back from the Sherriff's office to get my car out of the impound." I knew it! I guess after Lee was kicked out of the Key Club he staggered around with a coffee and then decided to get into his car and go home. On the way home he clipped some guy's car. The guy must have followed Lee, and at an intersection got out of his car and started yelling at Lee which led to an altercation which ensued with the Beverly Hills police showing up and carting Lee off to the Clinker. A few days later, I went into Studio City to meet Jamie for coffee at Starbucks on Ventura Boulevard. We were sitting outside and laughing about last Sunday night. Jamie and I started talking about my stalker. I swear a minute later, Jamie creeped me out.

"Dude, I think you're being watched."

"What?"

"Yeah, bro, she's there. You're being watched right now."

I turned around and sure enough, guess who was lurking a block away from me. Miss Obsessive made a beeline for me. She started talking to me with her twisted smile.

"Where the hell do you live?" I asked. She said she was from Granada Hills, which is miles and miles away from Studio City. Coincidence? I think not!

"What are you doing?" she asked me, trying to be all innocent and demure.

"Leaving!" I stood up and motioned to Jamie that we should split. As we walked to the parking lot, I whispered to him. "Is she following me?" I asked.

"Oh yeah. She's back there."

"Jamie, you've got to drive me around the block. I don't want this nut following me," I said. I didn't want her to see my car, even though a small part of me feared she already had. She caught up to us quickly and asked where I was going and when I would be performing again. I just ignored her. As I got into Jamie's SUV, she stood there staring at me.

Jamie took me around the block and dropped me off at my car. This chick had really freaked me out and I must have looked like I had seen a ghost. As I drove down Laurel Canyon I started to think "How is it that this chick pops up everywhere I am." I really was considering calling the police when I got home. It finally dawned on me. The night we did the live DVD shoot at the Whisky we had a Limo. I think she had waited outside and then followed the Limo back, which dropped me off in front of my place. It's the only thing that made sense.

At the beginning of July we headed to the East coast to do 6 shows and that would be the bulk of our work that summer. When I came back from that trip I really started analyzing my life and felt like I was living in this self absorbed bubble. I really started to pray a lot and I think God kept telling me to figure it out on my own. Around this time Adam had been going to these weekly AA and addiction meetings every Tuesday morning. I would have long conversations with Mike Duda about how fucked up we felt inside and questioned our addictions.

I decided to go to one of those meetings with Adam and of course Lee, since he had to go because of the DUI. The meetings were held at the bottom of the Key Club. I was nervous as hell but thought I will really try to take something from it. As we walked downstairs, Adam introduced me to these girls and one of the girls said to me in this creepy cheerleader cult voice "Are you ready to get sober!!" I was ready to leave already. I felt like I was at one of those Pentecostal churches where they try and ram it down your throat.

Adam Hamilton:
The years of living the rock and roll life had definitely caught up with us. It does with everyone eventually. Yet, some of us have made it through the war and are able to live normal lives. They can come off tour and not touch any booze and not have a problem putting it down. Not me. I knew that I had a problem and I knew I needed help. In April of 2006 I decided that I had had enough and went to my first twelve step meeting. I had tried quitting on my own but had no success. I thought why not check it out and see what it is all about. Hey, if it can work for guys who were my heroes and get them sober, it could work for me. It was scary at first because all I knew of sobriety was what I had seen in movies and they didn't make it look too cool. But, I knew I had to try something different and was willing to give it a go. I found the help I needed and made a commitment to sobriety. I realized that I was someone who needed to be sober to be happy. About this time, Stacey called me and had told me that he had been drinking too much and was starting to freak out. He said he might like to go check out a meeting with me. I think he saw that it was working for me and decided he might check it out for himself. Boy, were we surprised at how it went! Stacey being the good sport he is, went along with a good attitude and an open mind. But I could tell right away that it just might not be his thing. I think he got scared straight after that one meeting! It can work like that for some people. Those people are those who are not alcoholics. God bless em!

Raising Hell at the Rainbow -- Duda and I
-- New Years Eve '06

Mike Duda: WASP Bassist and Stacey's Friend

Somewhere around 2005 I met Blades! For lack of a better way to put it I was a fucking mess... I had just gotten out of a nightmare, dysfunctional, bullshit relationship that left me drained, burnt and ready for the all time bender of a lifetime....That being said the "Metal Blast Tour" was ready to hit the road. For LA Guns, Stephen Pearcy and WASP the timing was perfect... At the time I had been a member of Wasp for 10 years and no stranger to burning the candle at both ends......Around that time a buddy of mine, Joe Sutton asked me to hit the Greek Theater for Cinderella and Ratt. Totally not into it, I jumped at the chance to go and showed up fucking rotted!!!!! Hit will call, got the passes and ran to the bar. With beer in hand I here this voice, it was Stacey talking about how were going tour and how it was going to be a fucking blast. All I could focus on was why was this guy holding a cup of tea? ...So I asked and his reply was that he was fucking tanked the night before and was trying to get his shit together. I liked the guy right of the bat and I could tell Blades was a down to earth easy going guy with no hidden agenda. That's why to this day we are still great friends.
..And a common bond, the fact that we are both adopted, until you walk that walk people have no idea what it is like and how long it takes to come to grips with it, you are very lucky but at the same time very lost. It's been three years since that tour and life is

a lot different, a lot more calm. Well somewhat, I mean we are still rock stars. I have to say Stacey has become one of my best friends hanging out at the Coffee Bean shooting the shit and cracking jokes. I just can't say enough good stuff about the guy! Just a cool motherfucker....

As the meeting started more and more people indulged their addiction and alcohol problems. All I could think about was "Wow, are these people screwed up!" I really felt uncomfortable there and really realized that I was not an alcoholic at all and just suffered from self absorbed partying. I think Adam was laughing on the inside because he could see the sheer horror in my face by the end of the meeting. I called Mike and said "Dude that was some fucked up shit, I couldn't wait to get out of there." Mike was laughing his ass off as I played out a few of the scenarios of the meeting. I told Duda though, "You might want to go for yourself!" You will be able to tell right away if you have a problem. Really though the bottom line was, "We don't need those meetings but if you feel you need to go, I will go back with you." I think Mike was in deeper than me. Mike and I were two peas in a pod and I convinced him that we weren't addicts or alcoholics and that we just needed to channel our free time with other projects instead of going out and getting stupid. Of course a week later I was back at the Rainbow with Lee acting like a complete jackass downing two Corona's at the same time and chasing it with a shot while Lee egged me on.

Rock and Roll is one of the most dangerous jobs there is. It's so easy to fall into your own ego and become one with **"the** party" and start numbing yourself with drugs and alcohol. Most musicians have addictive personalities and it's easy to fall prey to such vices. Fortunately there are few that know when and where to clip it.

A NEW BEGINNING

Chapter 10

I finally started to get my shit together and with Lee going to alcohol classes and DUI classes we curtailed our partying. I had decided to try and repair my marriage and give it another shot. Lisa planned to move back in the early fall. Over the summer I had become good friends with one of my neighbors, Aaron, who worked at E! He told me was producing, writing and directing a music video for this female artist named Michelle Penn. I knew who Michelle was through a manager friend of mine. Aaron said "I need you to play a rock star." Hard stretch there huh! I suggested I just play myself. The shoot lasted three days and I had two different scenes. The first scene was Michelle and I in bed as her goofy boyfriend walked in on us. It was actually kind of tough and I realized I couldn't act worth a shit. I had to make-out with Michelle and it felt like I was kissing my sister. We must have done five or six takes on that alone. Then I had to act surprised and then have this "whatever" look on my face when he shrugged us off. I remember it was the beginning of August and it was hot as hell. Michelle had this house on top of this hill out by Dodger Stadium. That bedroom was like an oven especially with all the production lights. The second scene was a no brainer and we shot in Santa Monica. I basically just had to walk up to my car while the paparazzi snapped away and Michelle asks me for an autograph. Overall the video turned out great and I really liked the song as well.

There was this killer new venue in the heart of Hollywood called the Vine St. Lounge. It was a really neat place. It had this groovy lounge feel but had all these killer posters of Joan Jett, The New York Dolls and Iggy Pop up every where. We were scheduled to play there on August 18th. The turnout was great. Right before the show we had really fogged the place up! So we launch into the set and the fogger sets the fire alarm off. 118 decibels of shrieking blasts. Shit the Fire Department showed up and couldn't shut that fucker down! Well the show goes on. The alarm actually stopped for 30 seconds and then started up again. Now I've had some Spinal Tap moments, but this took the cake. After we finished the set, everyone in that place bolted! When we walked into the dressing room, I couldn't believe how bloody loud that alarm was. When I walked down into the bar it was like "Holy Shit is this thing blazing!" Hell if I was at that show I probably would have left after a few songs. I mean this alarm was really, really loud. After that show we parted ways with our manager and agent. I think we had tried to call him all week and he never once returned our calls?

At the end of August, Lisa had her car shipped out, (thank God) before she moved back. I picked her up at the airport. It felt good to have her back home and I think we were both a little nervous but felt like things were somewhat back to normal. I started to feel like I had a normal life again. Lee had decided to move to Las Vegas and I was bummed to see him go. That September we hooked up with Artist Representation and Management. They are a great agency and they are all musicians as well. We finally started working again that fall. The gigs were much bigger and better and we were finally back on the right track.

We played in Arkansas, Wisconsin, Minnesota, Illinois, Utah, and Pennsylvania. We finished up with a Texas run right before Christmas. I decided to get a much smaller tree for Christmas that year btw. Around this time I really started having problems with my bladder. I thought it was my prostate acting up again and all I could think about was having to go to a urologist and have to get that dreaded cyscoptopy. I was bloody miserable, especially when we were on the road. I was waking up every night having to pee. Sometimes I would wake up two or three times to piss and it wasn't much of a piss. It was almost impossible to pee when we were flying. If I didn't have an aisle set I would start having major anxiety. It ended up that I had gotten a UTI and by urinating so much, it had made my bladder shrink. Any ailment you could think of I had it! I was just grateful that I didn't have to go back to the urologist.

That winter we started to do exclusive shows with Warrant and Firehouse called the "*80's Invasion*." I thought it was a pretty good package, kind of diverse but still fun nonetheless. We were

scheduled to play an arena in Bloomington, Illinois. Now it had always been my dream to play an arena, and that was finally becoming a reality. I had accomplished a lot musically but had never played an arena. I would always hear Steve and Phil talk about big arena shows they would do back in the day. Anytime we were rolling in to a city somewhere and we passed the local arena, they would always talk about how they played there with so and so back in the day. I was always so envious when they would talk about that stuff. We had played this really great show just outside of Chicago the night before. That afternoon we rolled into Bloomington and checked into the Best Western. As we were waiting in the lobby of the hotel, the indoor pool was directly across from the lobby. There were all these overweight kids raising utter hell in the pool. Phil goes "Look there's a bunch of fat chubbies in the pool." At that point Adam and I noticed something a little different. Adam mutters quietly, "Dude, those are mentally handicap kids." We all looked at each other, turned red and laughed quietly. I guess there were a ton of disabled kids staying at the hotel for some convention. Later that afternoon we went to the arena for sound check. It was basically the back half of the arena that we were playing. But shit I didn't care, I couldn't wait. The pre sale was really good and I knew we were going to have an awesome night. After sound check we chilled in our dressing room which was a hockey dressing room. I was so used to playing night clubs, outdoor shows, and auditoriums, that this was all entirely new to me. After we ate the catered dinner, we started to get ready, as we were going on a 7 pm. We walked down the long corridor out to the side of the stage as the house lights went down. The stage was huge and it really was a different headspace. The sound was friggin of the hook. I just kept thinking, "Man I could get used to this". During "*Ballad of Jayne*" everybody got their lighters out. Right at that moment I realized that all the bullshit and hard work had all been worth it at that very moment. We partied that night and watched most of the rest of the show. As we were leaving Phil and I got on the Zamboni's (they are those big machines that clean the ice at a hockey game) and posed for a picture. As I was trying to sleep in my hotel room, I kept hearing tons of commotion coming from the hallways. It sounded like someone was bowling. Adam and I started laughing thinking that the handicap kids were firing each other down the stairway.

At the beginning of that winter Adam told us that he was going to leave the band but would fill in till we found someone. This news didn't really surprise us that much. We could tell Adam wanted to be in his studio working full time and didn't want to be on the road anymore. At the same time we were really bummed. Adam was our brother and brought a lot to the band. Before Adam had announced his departure, he was working with Poison in the studio while they recorded their "cover record" which was produced by Don Was. Don had taken a shine to Adam and was able to hook Adam up with a company called The Matrix. They basically have writers and producers working for them full-time. They offered Adam a full time job and it was right up his alley. We were really happy for Adam, but we were like "Shit we got to get someone really quickly or we're going to be off the road for a while," which meant no income. I immediately thought of my buddy Scotty Griffin, who was actually a guitar player but had been playing bass for quite some time in Dizzy Reed's band "Hookers and Blow". Scott and I met about a year earlier when Jizzy Pearl and I put together this all star cover band together called 100 Proof All Stars which also featured my buddy Mike Duda from WASP and Chris Slade from AC/DC. Scott was a great guy and talented musician. Scott had really been looking for a better gig as well. As soon as I called him he was like YES! We met with the rest of the band and set up an audition and Scott nailed it from the first note. We told Scott he got the gig and he was busting. I was glad we were able to get someone so quickly because the ad I had placed in the Recycler was producing people who were definitely not suited for the band. I remember this one guy who called me and said in a Romanian accent "I play progressive bass like Billy Sheehan and have heavy metal look".

Scott's first run with us was in Rochester, Buffalo and Canandaigua, New York. L.A. Guns definitely keeps a tight ship time wise. We have one rule: DON'T BE LATE! Anytime we would do fly-ins we would have a shuttle pick us up. The first stop would be at Steve's and the second stop would be at my place to get the rest of us. I don't think Scott realized when we said be there at 8 am it really meant be there at 7:45 am. Scott didn't show up until 8:20. Needless to say he got his ass chewed out!

Scott was really digging being in the band and it was good having him there too. Scott and I started to look like bookends. Hell even my mother mistook Scott for me when we were in Rochester. My parents came to the Rochester show which was at the Water St. Music Hall. It was a great show and my parents had a blast! I even recall my mom pumping her fists in the air!

Me and the Gunners with my Mom and Dad
---Rochester, April '07

A week after the NY run we flew into Vegas and then two days later we were heading over to Laughlin for three days to play the River Run festival with our good buddies Warrant. We had that first night in Vegas off and were playing the next night at this killer new club called Polyesters which was in the main floor of the Stratosphere Hotel and Casino. A night off in Vegas spells trouble.

Scott Griffin: L.A. Guns Bassist:

A lot of times when we have a string of dates, for the first day Stacey will say, "Dude, I'm taking it easy tonight. I'm just gonna have maybe one or two beers, I really have to pace myself for the rest of the shows." What this basically meant, is he's going to totally blow it out in true rock star fashion the first night.

Not only that, but Lee was now living in Vegas and we were all going to hook up and go out. Lee came by the hotel and took Scotty and I off to the Hard Rock in his new 'Jag. After three or four beers, I could see that look in Lee's eye like I had seen so many times, "Well Blades I'm going to get a Limo and we're going to raise some hell!" We went back to the hotel and grabbed Riley and Jeff our road manager. I knew we were in for a crazy night because Steve was with us and ready to party which was a rare treat. We had a Limo and Lee had called ahead and VIP'd all of us at 54 at the Luxor. Not only that but we had a camera crew with us documenting the whole trip. We were whisked upstairs and there is this huge table with buckets of beer, vodka and wine. Everybody in that damn place must have come by the table that night. Of course a "Black Haired" rock band and a camera crew does cause a little attention. That night started to become a blur and I remember Jeff dancing like a madman with some little oriental girl. We went back down to the limo, and went off to another bar. I don't really remember the rest of that night but do recall Lee having his shirt off and guzzling two beers at the same time while screaming, "I'm a professional!" The next day we were all hurting. There's nothing like walking through a casino totally hung over looking for something to eat. Scott and I met up at the pool on the top floor and sat in the hot tub and just whined like two little kids of how shitty we felt.

Polyesters was one of the neatest venues I've seen. They basically have four different rooms in the bar that are intertwined. They have a 70's, 80's (the big room) 90's and 2000 rooms. Each room was decorated with memorabilia from each era. It was a strange gig though because you could hear all the bleed through of the other music from each room. We had fun though and put on a really good show. The next day we left for Laughlin. It was a really close drive and we checked into this old style hotel that was right on the Colorado River. We were playing in the parking lot of the casino with Warrant for the Laughlin River Run Festival. It looked like it was going to be a fun three days. We were scheduled to play at 7 pm and it was like 101 degrees. When you play outside in that kind of heat you almost have to channel it out of your mind and just barrel through it. I had turned Scotty onto my famous Zombie Juice and we polished a few too many off that night. I remember lying in bed at four in the morning and it felt like I was having a heart attack. The Laughlin gig was cake. All the food and booze was covered and we just hung out by the pool, played for an hour at 7 pm and then just partied the rest of the night. There were these three complete lunatics from Australia that were the equivalent of "Bill and Ted." They were there all three nights and these guys rocked like no person I have ever seen. These guys were so rotted that it was like watching a three ring circus.

The second day, I hung out at the pool with Erik and Jerry from Warrant. It was hot as hell and I thought I would cool myself off with a dip in the pool. Let's just say there was more suntan lotion in that pool than there was chlorine. The next two nights were a blast and the attendance was great. Joey Allen and I would hold court in the back bar of the casino after the concert and act like a couple of high school kids.

Joey Allen--- Warrant Guitarist and Stacey's friend

I have laughed longer and harder with Stacey in the few years we have known each other than I have in decades spent with other friends. From the first time we shared a bill together we have gotten along famously, like brothers. In today's rock 'n' roll world that is a rarity and I cherish it. He has an incredible talent for playing guitar, entertaining his fans and holds the highest integrity with everything he is involved with.

After the three days, we were pretty burnt and ready to go home. We loaded up the van and headed back to Vegas to catch our flight home. The Vegas airport was a friggin zoo and we ended up missing our flight. We thankfully caught the next flight and got back to L.A.

As I lay in bed that night I felt like someone was stabbing my ear! Well that oil slicked pool had given me one hell of an ear infection. The next two months were miserable. I couldn't for the life of me get that damn fluid in my ear to drain, even with antibiotics. Not only that but I couldn't hear shit out of my right ear. I really drove my wife nuts because I couldn't hear anything she would say to me. Hell even after the fluid drained, my ear rang like a son of a bitch for a month. I actually fell into a depression and thought my right ear was fucked.

After the Nevada run we flew into Gillette, Wyoming. We took this tiny little plane from Denver. Anytime we do that Phil enjoys screwing with me. He knows how much I hate flying on small planes. Phil is actually a pilot himself. He would do stuff like, "Oh that sound isn't good, usually when you hear something like that, the propeller is about to explode." Of course he would be laughing under his breath as I had the fear of God on my face.

We had the night off in Gillette and we were staying at this huge Clarion Hotel that had this enormous atrium in it. Jeff, Phil, Scotty and myself decided to go up to the hotel bar for a few beers after dinner. Half of the bar was decorated in balloons. I guess someone was having a small bachelorette party. After a half an hour or so, this guy comes over to the table wanting to take pictures with us and the rest of the bachelorette party. We really weren't in the mood and nicely told him maybe later. Sometime before that this goofball fraternity type jerk came by the table and does the metal sign to us and leaves. The guy who wanted pictures must have gone back to his party and told everybody that we were not taking any pictures and that we were a bunch of jerks. Mr. Frat Boy comes storming up to the table and slams a dildo down on the table and yells "That's what I think of you guys." That short fuse in me snapped and I wanted to kick his frat boy ass all the way back to his campus. I stood up and yelled, "Hey Buddy, come back and pickup your bath toy!!!" What was funny is that the dildo stuck to the table and was wavering like a metronome. Phil stood up and grabbed the dildo and threw it back at him. However he missed him completely and clocked some lady in the back of the head. All hell broke loose and this tame little bachelorette party turned into an angry lynch mob. They kept yelling "Don't mess with the locals!"

That spring we hooked up with a promoter we affectionately titled "Buffalo Bob." We started working with Bob quite a bit. Bob is killer and one of the best promoters we have ever worked with. Bob is a huge L.A. Guns fan! Anytime we did a run with Bob, we would be treated like royalty. He would pick us up with limos and we always stayed in five star hotels. I'll never forget when we were in Long Island, NY. Bob took us to this really ritzy steakhouse for dinner. We looked so out of place there. He must have dropped a grand on the dinner alone. I've never seen so much sushi and seafood appetizers in my life. We were so stuffed that by the time our steaks came, we could barely finish them. We were all trying to force feed these 30 dollar filets down. It was like that scene in the *"Great Outdoors"* with John Candy. I actually felt drunk off all the protein from the steak and seafood. During dinner, Bob broke out gifts for everybody. He had this girl design a new backdrop for us and had all the waiters unfold the thing and hold it up. I think everyone in that restaurant was looking at our table. Bob was like a big kid around us and lived it up for three or four days before going back to his wife and kids.

That summer was killer. We did some really great outdoor shows with Warrant and Firehouse. We had done this run in Upstate NY and on the last night, Phil and I had to leave at four in the morning and go to Buffalo to catch a plane to Green Bay, WI. Phil and I were doing a three day stint at the Oneida Casino with the Hollywood Vampires. HV was a cool little side project with Brent Woods and Muddy Stardust. It was a cake gig. Three days at the Radisson, which was totally comp'd along with all our food and booze. We only had to play an hour set and the money was really, really good. As Phil and I were waiting at the gate at the Buffalo airport, the gate clerk couldn't find Phil's name on our flight. It ended up Phil was on a different flight altogether! By the time we figured this out I only had a half an hour to catch my flight! The security line was of course a mile long. I finally got through security and the gate was all the way at the other end, of course just my luck. I hadn't been to bed yet! I must have looked like hell running through the airport with my pedal board and carry on bag huffing and puffing. My flight was connecting in Cincinnati. Pretty ridiculous just to go from Buffalo to Green Bay. I fell asleep on the plane and was woken up by the pilot saying that they were being diverted to Pittsburgh 'cause the radar was offline in Cincinnati. I was like "This has got to be a joke!" Only this shit would happen to me of course. It dawned on me then that my day just got completely fucked. We sat in Pittsburgh for 45 minutes and finally headed to Cincinnati. I knew I had missed my connection. I had to go to the Delta check in counter where they proceeded to tell me that the next flight was at 8 pm! Now I was supposed to land in Green Bay at 1:30 pm and was playing that night at 7 pm I was like, "Lady, you got to get me into Green Bay. I'm playing tonight!"

"I can get you to Milwaukee," she says.

Hi, I'm Planet Earth, have we met?

It looked like I was going to have to fly through Chicago and then connect to Green Bay. This was slowly turning into a nightmare. I was flipping and headed straight to the bar.

"How's it going?" the bartender asked.

"Not too good. Gimme a Corona!" The bartender frowned at my request and said

"Well I hate to make your day worse, but we aren't serving alcohol Right now." "Am I on a hidden camera show or something!"

Brent Woods had called me and said that his flight from L.A. had been cancelled and he had to divert through Chicago as well. As I got off the plane in Chicago I was totally fried by this point. They were unloading the small plane and I thankfully saw my guitars. I walked up to one of the baggage handlers and said "Is that big black bag showing it's going to Green Bay?" Yes he said. At least I knew my axes had the right tags on them. So many times when you have connections your shit can get lost very easily. I met up with Brent at the bar by our gate and slammed a cold beer and starting laughing. What a fuckin' day I was having. We flew over to Green Bay in no time and it was about 4:30 at this point. My good friend Selene who was living near Green Bay met me at the airport with her friend. As we were waiting by the carousel for my guitars it was starting to take kind of long. I started to get nervous. Brent, Selene and Jamie were on the other side. I guess Brent said to Selene "Watch, this carousel is going to go around one more time and stop and Stacey is going to flip!" Sure enough the carousel stopped and my guitars were nowhere in sight! That was it, I snapped! I was so done with this day; I was ready to go back to L.A. Fortunately the casino was across the street from the airport. Poor Selene was walking on eggshells around me. I was fucking livid and no, definitely not much fun to be around. I got checked in. Of course Phil had been there since 1:30. At least I had this palatial room. The airline called me an hour later and said they were sending over my guitars. Of course you would think that would put me at ease, but when I opened up the case to my Les Paul Custom the main volume pot was sheered off! I couldn't believe that this day was just one constant screw you! I was so out of it I don't really remember playing and I think I passed out in my room at 9 pm with a steak sandwich in my hand. Phil and I and the rest of the band still laugh at the text message I left him when I landed in Green Bay-------NO GUITARS!!!!

I laugh about it now, but fuck that day was a bitch and would not want to experience something like that again. The next two days were a lot of fun. However, no rest for the wicked. On that fourth day Phil and I were flying back to L.A. and didn't get in till 11 pm. LAX was an absolute zoo and it took us an hour and a half to get out of there. The next morning we were being picked up at 9 am to head right back to LAX to fly into Twin Falls, Idaho for a big outdoor show with Warrant and Firehouse. Thankfully we had that night off in Twin Falls. Of course I got dragged to this bar with the promotion staff from Kruzer's. I remember Joey Allen calling me on my cell phone as I was chilling in my hotel suite and I could barely form a sentence. Joey started laughing "Dude, are you alright?"

DOWN UNDER

CHAPTER 11

The rest of that summer was a blast and it was great hanging with our buddies in Warrant. We would play Indianapolis for the first time in years. That show was really spectacular. We played at this huge nightclub and packed the place. The next morning we were flying into JFK to play at the resurrected famous L'Amours. That was a long ass day. It took us two hours from the airport just to get to Staten Island. After a very long sound check, they took us to one of the worst hotels I have ever stayed in. I couldn't believe that they had booked us into such a dump! Hell, they didn't even have a remote for the television, which didn't matter 'cause there was only two stations that came in anyways. Scotty and I had to share this piece of shit room together. You didn't even want to lay on the beds and the towels in the bathroom were like sandpaper. The only saving grace of the day was the club owner's wife cooking us an authentic Italian meal. They brought over huge trays of pasta, chicken parmigiano and loaves of Italian bread. We all gorged ourselves and it was a meal fit for a mob. That night Eddie Trunk came out and hung with us and also introduced us. The next day we had a late flight, so we thought we would be able to sleep in, WRONG! This front desk asshole started calling all the rooms at 10:30 am telling us in his nasty New York accent, to get the hell out of the rooms. This guy must have called us every five minutes. I wanted to go downstairs and drag that prick out from under his desk and pummel him. While we were waiting downstairs, this clerk was even banging on people's door yelling "Get the hell out of the room we got people waiting to check in!" Who the fuck was waiting to check into this fleabag? If you are ever in Staten Island don't ever stay at the Victoria Crown Motor Lodge.

That summer also saw us play in Sturgis, South Dakota for the first time. As you know Sturgis is the biggest and best bike rally festival in America. There was a new outdoor venue called the Boneyard and they were having concerts every night of the week. They had everyone from Blue Oyster Cult to Foghat, Dokken and Quiet Riot to name a few. We flew into South Dakota that morning and were picked up in a limo with no air conditioning. After we checked into the hotel in Rapid City we then had to grab our stuff and head over to the concert grounds. They picked us up in another limo; at least this one had A.C. It took almost 50 minutes just to get to the Boneyard. We were playing that night with Warrant and Firehouse. We of course had the shit time slot of 8pm. It was a huge stage, with these massive video screens on both sides. I thought "Man this is going to be killer!" After we sound checked we walked back to the big house on wheels that was our dressing room and got ready. It was still sunny out and as we walked up to the stage there was nobody around! Where the hell are all the people! The place was so big that there were lots of people scattered around, just not in front of the stage. The whole set I just pretty much watched myself on the jumbo tron. Of course by the time Warrant went on it was fuckin packed! Nevertheless we had fun hanging out and partied with the Warrant boys afterwards. Scott and I would always be the last ones to leave. We had to cram 7 people into this small limo for the 45 minute ride back to the hotel in Rapid City. Jamie St. James and I were totally buzzed and were cracking each other up so hard on the way back that we were both in tears pissing ourselves. Jamie is a great guy and I never realized how funny he was.

Scott was a complete maniac and totally enjoyed being in L.A. Guns and on the road. He reminded me a little of myself when I first joined the band except multiplied by ten times. That guy would savor every second

Scott Griffin:
Stacey believes in what he believes in and there isn't anybody who can change his mind. We were driving to some gig in a van one day and we started talking about the old Cathouse. Stacey started in about how there needs to be something like that now to bring it all back. We were going on about this for a while till Phil finally said, "Look Stacey, it ain't ever gonna come back like it once was." We both reluctantly nodded in agreement. It got very quiet. While I accepted Phil's assessment as matter of fact and was onto thinking about something completely different, I happened to glance over at Stacey who was staring out the window with this look in his eyes that seemed to me as though he was saying, "Oh, it can happen, fuck yeah it can..."

of the day and party his ass off. How he survived on three or four hours of sleep a night was beyond me. There was many a time that I would have to drag Scotty out of the bar. He's so rock n'roll!

The following week we would be heading back to the Dakotas to do more shows with Firehouse and Skid Row. The last show of the summer we played at this amazing casino resort called Prairie Knights. The place was in the middle of nowhere and I mean nowhere. We couldn't find the place and we assumed we were lost. I remember we had come to this crossroads and were flipping quarters to decide if we should turn left or right? Plus, no one could get a signal on their cell phones. Fortunately, someone drove up behind us and directed us the right way. Out of nowhere like a mirage appeared this massive casino. This place was really cool and the venue we were playing in was like a mini arena. It was great to catch up with the Skids guys. Everybody who worked at the hotel asked us for autographs. I don't think they got too many rock stars come through that way. The place was packed and we really put on a kick ass show. It was a great way to end the summer.

That fall we were going to be going to Australia for the first time ever. We would be doing four shows in six days. We were going to play Brisbane, Sydney, Melbourne and Adelaide. I was surprised that L.A. Guns had never been there to play, especially back in the late 80's. We were all very excited about the tour and the continent down under was ready for us. We were flying Qantas and had an 11 pm flight. We were all trying to gear up for the

14 hour flight. I didn't care 'cause I was so excited to be going. The flight was long as hell and there was hardly any leg room. Scott and I tossed and twisted the whole flight! I don't think I slept much at all and my ass was numb for sitting so long. Justin Timberlake was on our flight and so were all his staff. There had to be at least 50 or more of these employees. I wondered "What the hell do all these people do for this guy?" After 13 hours of boredom we made an unscheduled stop in Fiji. It was pretty weird; I mean how many times can you say you spent an hour in Fiji. We weren't allowed to de-board the plane so the best thing to do was get up and stretch. After we took off we still had another three hours to bloody fly. All in all it turned out to be about a 16 hour flight. We landed in Brisbane and cleared through customs like a breeze. The weather was gorgeous and the tour manager Brent Metal picked us up. It was so surreal, we were actually in Australia. We drove towards downtown and pulled into this beautiful condo type hotel right on the water. We checked in and headed up to our rooms which were pristine. They were all suites with balconies that overlooked the water and downtown.

Across the hotel was this little café that we sat and ate pizza and sampled some of Australia's finest beers. We were all completely whacked with jet lag but we were really enjoying the day. After lunch I settled back in my room and crashed for a few hours. Later that afternoon I walked down to the waterfront and watched the sunset. Brisbane reminded me a lot of South Florida. Scott and I decided to go out that night since we were off and check out the sights. As I was waiting for Scott I was sitting on my balcony and saw the hugest bat I had ever seen in my life. I swear the wingspan on this thing was four feet! I darted back into the room after seeing that thing. Bats give me the creeps. Brisbane is surrounded by water and they have all these water taxis everywhere. Scott and I trolled down to the waterfront and took the water taxi across the inlet to downtown. Scott and I were practically high fiving each other because it really felt like we had accomplished something touring on the other side of the planet. We walked around downtown and couldn't find shit. I guess we were in the wrong area for the nightlife. We finally figured out where to go and hopped in a cab. We hit a few bars and it wasn't long before we were recognized and were having drinks bought for us. The Australian people are very cool, outgoing and friendly. The Aussies were really tripping on us. Jeff met up with us and we hit a few more hot spots. By two in the morning I was really starting to feel the jet lag. Scotty and I took a cab back and realized I had already spent a hundred bucks, on what I don't know. Australia is very expensive. Scott and I raided the mini bar and had one last beer out on the balcony. It was about 3:30 at this point and I was more than ready to crash!

I slept like a rock and was woken up out of the blue by the phone at 11 am. "Yo Stace it's Scotty, want to grab some breakfast" I was like "Uuuuuuuuggghheeeeeeeeeerrrrrrrr No" I was sleeping so good and had a hard time falling back asleep. I finally fell asleep for a couple hours later on. We weren't sound checking till 5:30 and I sat around my room going crazy. We finally went to the venue and sound checked. I had noticed this door by the dressing room that had a pane of broken glass in the middle of it. I thought to myself "Someone is going to cut their hand on that shit!" After the check we headed back to the hotel. I decided to order a pizza and they told me it was going to be an hour. Australia has a very relaxed attitude. I said "An hour for a pizza?" the Pizza Hut guy goes (insert Australian accent) "No worries mate, It's alright it will get there" I replied "Crikey." That first night was great. The show was packed and it got hot as hell! As we were walking out of the dressing room to do the meet and greet, we had to pass through that door with the broken glass. As we got to the merchandise table, I could see Steve grabbing his hand with this look of agony! I knew someone was going to cut their hand on that door! Unfortunately it was my drummer. Steve was flipping and rightfully so! I couldn't believe it, there was that force again. Steve cut his hand really bad and I thought "Well, that was a fun tour."

 The next morning we were flying to Sydney. We were touring with this Australian band called Head Inc. We were checking in twenty two pieces at the airport 45 minutes before the flight. As I said the Aussies were pretty relaxed. We on the other hand were getting nervous, "Uh guys don't you think we should hurry up!" Again "No worries mate!" Of course all the oversized items didn't make that flight to Sydney. I think they realized that we needed a little more time to check in after that.

Steve had to be taken to the hospital and have the wound in his hand cauterized to stop the bleeding. Steve's hand looked like "The Mummy."

Sydney Harbor Front—Australia Tour –Oct. '07

Sydney was incredible. We played a packed house at the Manning University. It was only two days into the tour and Jeff was already starting to crack! Then again the poor guy was worked into a nub over the last few days. It was hilarious when he snapped. As him and the monitor guy were getting ready to pull the curtain back, Jeff was cursing at the guy and Phil's microphone was picking up every syllable. We were like "Dude shut up!" That night was a blast and we were really on fire. The meet and greet was insane and we moved so much merchandise. Later that night we sat outside the Holiday Inn knocking back a few beers with D.W. the main Australian promoter and a few fans.

The next morning we were off and running again. When we arrived in Melbourne there were quite a few young kids waiting for us, as there were in Sydney when we got off the plane. We really dug that, and it was the first time I ever had fans waiting at an airport for pictures and autographs. Melbourne was totally different. It really had an English feel to it. The show was really packed and the meet and greet lasted over 2 hours! During the meet and greet I could have sworn I was in England. By this time of the tour I was really starting to feel burnt, the jet lag, late nights and early mornings were really catching up with me.

We were in the last stretch of the tour and we flew to Adelaide for the final show. It was really weird, we were flying into South Australia over the Indian Ocean and realized just how far away from home we were. Of course there had to be drama the last day just like there always was! Steve of all people didn't get his luggage and it was a kick in the nuts especially after the poor guy got his hand all tore up. Poor Steve was starting to boil over. We all felt so bad for the guy. I guess his bag was sent to Perth which was all the way on the west side of the continent. I knew Steve wasn't going to see his bag till we got back to L.A. This, of course, is exactly what happened. That helpless feeling sucks!

I think I had the most fun in Adelaide. The show was amazing and there were tons of young rockers. Every time I would come to the front of the stage, this 17- year- old girl would grab my nuts. I couldn't believe my eyes when I looked to stage left and saw the motions of "Bill and Ted" It was those crazy fuckers that were in

Laughlin. I high fived all three of them, those guys were really a hoot.

As we were leaving the venue I remember there was this rocker kid who followed us to one of the vans and climbed in with us. I thought who the hell is this and just assumed it was a friend of D.W's or something. This kid then follows me into my room. I was like who are you? And why are you in my room. Over the next hour, every five minutes some kid was knocking on my door while Phil and I drank a cold beer. We had caught wind of this party going on at this after hours club a block away from the hotel. Phil and I figured we might as well stay up all night since we had to leave at 8 am. Phil and I wandered over to this club and the place was raging! It was filled with young rock and rollers raising hell. It kind of reminded me of the old Cathouse in L.A. We basically had carte blanche in this place and a lot of the kids were freaking out that we were hanging there. I think we stayed until about 5 am. I decided to go back to my hotel and there were still kids banging on my door. I'm not sure how all these kids found out where we were staying, let alone which room number. I sat in the shower for the next hour and mentally prepared for the travel day we had ahead of us. We had to fly from Adelaide to Sydney, then the 14 hour flight home back to L.A. I think I slept the whole way on the flight from Sydney.

We did a one off Thanksgiving show in Minneapolis with Vince Neil. We played at this beautiful big club called the Myth. The show was fantastic, about 1800 people and it was really cool to meet and hangout with Vince. Of course I had to tell him how "*Shout at the Devil*" changed my life at the age of 15, hahaha.

Two weeks later Lisa and I did our usual Christmas tree purchase at Home Depot. Only in Hollywood can you wait in line with your tree while some lunatic homeless person is walking around the tree lot with a lighter saying he's going start a fire. I don't know what it is with me and Christmas trees, but I have the worst damn luck with those things. When we had bought the tree it was a little uneven on the stump. Lisa and I waited in line with about 11 people in front of us to get it cut evenly. I'll be the first to admit I have the patience of a 12- year- old brat. After half an hour I was fed up and said, "Screw this, the tree will be fine the way it is." Boy could I have not been more wrong. I must have wrestled with that tree and the stand for about two hours! As soon as I would get the tree somewhat centered with the tree stand screws, I would crawl out from under the tree with needles in my hair and sap all over my hands only to walk away and then lunge for it as it tipped over time and time again! Picture my skinny ass lurching for a seven foot pine tree. Lisa and I were of course screaming and yelling at each other the whole time. Why the fuck didn't I just wait and get the stump evened out! I grabbed the tree and said, "That's it! This fucker is going in the dumpster! I think a good "Christmas Angel" came to my rescue. As I grabbed the tree it finally stayed in place. Of course it was crooked as shit but it stayed in place.

The following weekend we attended Bobby Blotzer's Christmas party. Bobby had a killer new house up by Magic Mountain in Castaic and Lisa and I had a blast drinking and hanging with Corabi, Brent Woods, Jon Levin and some of Bobby's friends. As the party was winding down around 3 am, we were getting ready to leave and Blotz says "Dude where you going? My buddy from Magic Castle is about to lay out some sick ass magic tricks". I'm glad we stayed coz this guy did some of the craziest magic I've ever seen. He would have a deck of cards and then have Lisa pull out a card. He then would have her write her name on the card and then shuffle the deck. He then would pull out this Altoids box and then gave it to Lisa. She opened it up and the fuckin card was in there with her name on it. He then puts the card back in the Altoids box and does this weird shit with his hand and then takes his shoe off and the same fuckin card is in the bottom of his shoe! Blotz you know how to throw a party dude!

We finished the rest of the year off with a show in Vegas at this new club called the Rok Bar. We decided to rent a van and drive to the gig with all the wives. We figured it would be a great weekend and we were all staying at the "Hooters Hotel and Casino". As we were heading onto the 15 into Nevada, Steve saw a CHP pull up behind us with his lights on. As we were pulling over it dawned on us that nobody had their seat belts on and that's indeed why we were being pulled over. As the officer walked over to our vehicle; almost all of us simultaneously buckled up. The CHP officer blurted out "A little too late for that don't you think!" He was about to give all of us a 200 hundred plus dollar ticket when Steve smartly said "Hey we're L.A. Guns and we are on our way to play in Vegas." The cop actually said "No Shit? You guys are really L.A. Guns?" It literally saved our asses and he gave us just a warning. Thank God for name dropping.

IN THE MIX

CHAPTER 12

New Years started off with a bang. We celebrated with a small New Years Eve party over Jon Levin's Brentwood condo. As I knocked back Coronas with Vikk Foxx and some mutual friends, I felt that needy alcoholic demon start to raise it's ugly head again. As the party started to wind down around 1 am, I was just getting started. I insisted that Lisa and a few friends go to the Cat Club. I knew my buddy Kenny who tended bar there would certainly pour cold beers down my throat. One of Lisa's friends was unsure of going and she had driven us to the party. I didn't take no for an answer and basically pissed her off enough that she finally said "FINE!" The rest of the night I don't remember and I'm pretty positive I pissed a few people off including my wife. I couldn't understand it; I used to be a fun person to be around when I would party. However, more and more I was turning into a selfish prick when I drank.

The NAMM show was coming up and Phil, Scott and I were scheduled to do a signing at the Crate Amplifier booth. It was a fun day but draining nevertheless. My goal that year was to score an endorsement with the guys at Jackson Guitars. It was the end of the day on Friday and I finally made my way upstairs to the Fender booth. Fender now owns Jackson and Charvel guitars. I met with Mike Kotzen from Jackson and really hit it off with him. After a few phone calls, Mike invited me down to the Fender factory and gave me the factory tour which eventually led to the endorsement after talking with Chris and Brian in the Artists department.

Jamming on a new Charvel at the Fender Factory '08

The next night after NAMM we were kicking off the 20th Anniversary tour at the Whisky. I knew we were in for a great night because we knew there was a ton of people from out of town coming to see us. That night exceeded my expectations. Not only did we play great but we sold out the club by 10pm. They were actually turning a ton of people away. There was just something really special about that night. The *L.A. Times* came out to do a feature on us and original bassist Kelly Nickels came up and played two songs with us. When Phil introduced Kelly the place went nuts.

Kelly, Scott, Steve, Phil and I - No Mercy at the Whisky-'08

A few days after the Whisky show we left for a run up in Michigan and Ohio. We played the beautiful Emerald Theater in Mt. Clemens, Michigan. I had worked up this really cool guitar solo.

I played for a couple of minutes by myself, and then I would kick into this funky riff where the band kicked in and I played lead over that. It went great at the Whisky. That night in Mt. Clemens it did not. After a minute or so, the rig I was using started to cut out every other second. Now only this shit would happen to me when I was the only one playing of course. My tech finally came over and fixed the situation. I guess my instrument cable came a little loose out of my guitar. Like I said, only that shit would happen to me in the middle of a 'solo.'

The next three nights in Cleveland, Cincinnati, and Toledo were amazing. The band was starting off the year right and really pulling respective numbers. The best night out of that week surprisingly was Toledo. We played this huge place and it was packed. There were lots of young people there too. They had these go-go dancers in cages on each side of the stage. Very distracting for sure!

The following week we left for New York for four shows on the east coast. Thankfully we were flying out of Burbank on good ole Jet Blue. Dan Rather was actually on our flight. I'm still mad at myself for not saying hello to him. We played in Jersey, Hartford, CT, Factoryville, PA and a show with Slaughter in Long Island. The show in Pennsylvania was interesting. It would be the first time in my career where I fell down on stage. Halfway through the set I was back stepping and my cable wound around my right leg like a noose and down I went. Now I just didn't fall down, I went kidney first into the drum riser! Steve said that he actually felt the riser move. I fuckin saw stars let me tell you! I got up and walked off to the side stage and just stood there not playing anything so I could catch my breath. Our good ol' bud Buffalo Bob was with us and we headed back to New York for the final show with Slaughter. Like I said earlier Bob was the bomb and treated us like kings. He showed up in Factoryville with a brand new USA Fender Telecaster for Phil!

We were playing at the Crazy Donkey in Long Island and stayed at the same Hilton we were at last summer. The show at the Donkey was packed and for a bitter cold Sunday night, that was pretty cool! We kicked ass and Scotty and I watched the Slaughter boys from side stage. The guys in Slaughter had a ton of people back to the Hilton. Loud drunk chicks, thin walls and the ritzy Hilton spell trouble. Bob had bought most of the rooms for LA Guns and Slaughter. All it took was one complaint and security was there in a flash. This guy wasn't fucking around either. These girls got more out of control and the cops ended up showing up. All I could think was, fuck I hope we don't get kicked out into the cold at 2 am.

The next morning we were flying back out of JFK home. It was so windy and cold it was like getting bitch slapped with a frozen 10 pound trout.

It was good to get back home to sunny southern California. Once again the following week we were off and running again. We had four shows in Texas. As soon as we got to Austin, Steve started getting sick. Now if someone in the band starts to get the flu, you can bank on someone else in the band getting sick as well. Of course that being me! Now this was a special knock down, drag out flu and it was a shit kicker let me tell you. I caught it the last night in El Paso, but Steve had it for the whole week. How he played every night was beyond me. Steve had that damn thing for three weeks! Texas is always fun and the shows in San Antonio and El Paso were off the hook. The El Paso show was borderline insane. The Texans and Mexicans like their metal for sure!

We continued to tour over the next month in Utah, Colorado, NY and a spectacular show in Boston. Of course it's Steve's home town. The band was on fire and drawing great numbers. As much drama and turmoil as there was on the road, those 90 minutes couldn't have been more fun every night and brought the four of us even closer.

A few months earlier in the beginning of February, I launched my new nightclub with promoter Julian Douglas called Voodoo Hollywood. During the prior summer I had this idea for a rock and roll club that would be reminiscent of the old Cathouse. I had told Julian that I wanted to start a new night in Hollywood that would attract a lot of the people who were going to the Key Club on Monday nights to see *Metal Skool*. I thought if I could get a lot of those younger people who were into the 80's metal, we would have a really cool night. Julian had come up with this idea for a New Orleans type of vibe night and had a place set up for a Tuesday night. So we combined the two ideas and Voodoo Hollywood was born. We started to get a really amazing response to the new night and thought we were going to be very successful, but once again I ended up rolling snake eyes. The club was into its 12th week and the two of us had not made a fuckin cent! So much for new business ventures. The night just never caught on, no matter what we tried. There were times when we would have like 12 people in the bar. The owners, as cool as they are, I think they started to rethink the whole idea of having this night in their club. Shit, even on our busy nights (what few there were), we didn't even make any money. I basically just showed up most Tuesdays and paced back and forth while drinking Coronas all night for free pondering "Why the hell isn't anybody showing up?"

Earlier in the year I had gotten to know a woman named Denise Ames. Denise was *"Thee Media Chick of L.A."* She has her own TV show called *"Focus in the Mix"* and is very successful. Denise's show is kind of like *Entertainment Tonight* but more well rounded, not just featuring actors but musicians and politicians alike. Denise is a big L.A. Guns fan and had taken a liking to the band. She had asked if Scott and I would be her celebrity guests on one of her shows. I thought this would be great because we could pump the hell out of the band and Denise's show had a large viewing audience. The show was fantastic and ended being the biggest selling DVD of *"Focus In the Mix"* for 2008.

Denise Ames: *Host of Focus in the Mix and Stacey's good friend*
Being around the music industry for decades, I find it extremely rare for fans to follow a musician's career in every move he makes. Stacey's do, as this was apparent in the incredible response across the globe to his on camera interview on my TV show. Not only does he possess

good looks along with undeniable charisma both on stage and off, but also a brilliant mind on so many levels; all of which came across quite clearly during his interview with me, much to his fans' delight. Stacey is a phenomenal musician yet humble about what he does for a living; rockin' the planet kickin' ass with (the real) L.A. Guns. He truly is one of the most beautiful human beings I have ever known, inside and out. The music industry wouldn't be quite as 'metal' without him!"

"Focus in the Mix TV Show"- Denise, Heidi, Me and Daisy-'08

It has been a blast hanging with Denise at her studio. Over the last few months I have met and hung out with people like Lol Tolhurst and Micheal Dempsey from The Cure, Gretchen Bonaduce and Daisy De La Hoya from Bret Micheals' *"Rock of Love 2."*

One night after eating dinner, I hopped on my computer and checked my Myspace page. There were a few messages in my inbox. The first one was kind of strange, no picture and no name and the message titled "Hello from the past." I was hesitant to open it up. The message was from Angie! I about fell out my chair. I couldn't believe it! I hadn't talked to Angie since she had dumped me almost 10 years ago. The message read something like "Hey Stace it's Angie, just dropping by to say hello and it's awesome you've ended up where you are." It really tripped me out to hear from her. I mean I thought I would never talk to Angie again for the rest of my life. At the same time I felt all that pain that she had caused me come to the surface. I decided to email her back. It was good to talk to her again and clear some much needed water under the bridge. Angie sure enough had stayed with that lunatic she started seeing after me and ended up marrying him and they also had a kid together. She confided that she had made a mess of her life and was separated from her husband. After a few more emails I was able to put the past to rest between us and I'm glad I contacted her back.

Angie:

"I'm so sorry for hurting you. It's a trip to think that you really loved me like that. I don't know what was wrong with me - I WAS having the time of my life. Was it really Valentine's Day? That wasn't on purpose. Something in me freaked out with almost 2 years of drama-free, laughing until I pee myself times with you. I never laughed so hard! You were so funny. I definitely loved you then and it scared the shit out of me."

The emails however got shorter and farther apart and she took me off of her friends list on Myspace and then deleted her page completely. Angie seemed to be distancing herself from me one more time. It was sad to see that her estranged husband still had that much control over her. Hey, maybe I'll talk to her in another ten years.

ALL ROADS LEAD HERE
CHAPTER 13

Once again we hit the ground running. I was really starting to enjoy touring at the start of spring. We continued to draw really well. We did a big east coast run that saw us in New York and Mass. We played L'Amours again and really packed the place and no, we did not stay at the Victoria Crown Motor Lodge. It was nice to stay at the Marriott in Staten Island but a pain in the ass getting to and from the club. We also played right in the heart of Boston and of course Steve's brothers came out. I always looked forward to seeing those two and they were always a fuckin riot to be around. The following week we were heading up to northern California for two shows. We hadn't played up there in years because it usually sucks. The Friday night we played at the Hard Rock Café in Sacramento. I was blown away how good that show was and packed it was. It was a usual night and staff was extra attentive. At the end of the night the manager handed a piece of a paper to Steve. As Steve walked towards Phil and I in the dressing room I knew something wasn't right in Denmark. Steve goes, "I just got handed a fuckin bill for $180.00 for booze!" We were like "What!" The Hard Rock actually charged us for beer and wine. This was a first. Did they do this to every national band or were they trying to fuck us. I'm not sure but it was utter bullshit. The next night was another interesting one as well. We played in Walnut Creek and once again I was pleasantly surprised how great the turnout was. I was convinced the band was experiencing a second wind. Anyways, some dude was smoking a joint near the dressing room and security and the owner caught wind of it and blamed us. They started freaking on us and one of the dipshit security guys who looked like Lumpy from "*Leave it to Beaver*" started getting 'agro' as I said "Lighten up Francis." I guess that didn't sit well with him. The owner, who looked like Yukon Jack told us to get the "fuck out!" I don't know who the bigger asshole was, Lumpy or Yukon, hahaha.

A few weeks after, Phil and I were gearing to head back to the good ole' Oneida Casino in Green Bay, Wisconsin. We were going to do three nights there acoustically in the Casino Lounge. We flew into Minneapolis and connected to Green Bay. I know what you're thinking, I got there with no delays or having to take four flights. Phil and I were excited about the week and had only done the acoustic thing once or twice before. It was such a cake gig, play for one hour a night at 7 pm and just chill the rest of the time. We got into the Radisson/Oneida on Saturday night and were going to play Sunday, Monday and Tuesday night. This gig was great but you had nothing but time on your hands. I ended up drinking every night because there was literally nothing else to do. The shows went great and the stuff we played sounded really amazing. Our set was mostly L.A. Guns stuff and we also threw a few covers in like "*Walkin the Dog*" and "*Ziggy Stardust.*" Hell, we got standing ovations on the last two nights. By the third night I was ready to get out of there. We had been there for four days and I felt like I was living there. Anymore nights of eating Pizza and turkey croissant sandwiches at two in the morning I was going to have call Jenny Craig.

Phil and I had to get up at 7 am to catch the early flight out of Green Bay to Minneapolis and home. Now it didn't end there, oh no. We basically came home for less than an hour and were heading right back to the airport to fly to Mexico for 2 shows. By the time I got home I was baked. I turned into a raging asshole as I tried to shower, re-pack, eat and get ready in 45 minutes. We were flying Aero Mexico later that afternoon to Monterrey Mexico. As we were ready to board the plane the flight crew walked passed us and looked us up and down. A minute later the gate clerk came up to us and told us we couldn't board the plane wearing tank tops. I guess that's some kind of Mexican rule because you can't wear a tank top at El Compadre (one of Hollywood's most popular Mexican restaurants). The flight was great and I finally un-wound with a few complimentary Mexican beers. Most of the other people on the flight were excited that we were on the plane and the flight practically turned into a meet and greet. One of the pilots was this young female who looked a little like Shakira. She actually came out and sat next to Scotty and was flirting with him big time. No one can resist "Scotty Hollywood," hahaha.

After we got checked into the hotel, Scotty and I did a beer run with the promoters. I couldn't help but notice that there were cops everywhere pulling people over. Of course as soon as we pulled out of the liquor store we saw the flashing lights behind us. The cops let us go but I guess they figured if we made the stop for beer whoever was behind the wheel was under the influence. Then again we were in Mexico. Scotty and I hung out by the pool and downed a few Tecates. By this time it was two in the morning central time and I had been on the move for almost 24 hours. I was fried and headed up to my suite for some much needed rest.

The next day we headed over to the venue that afternoon and sound checked. The bar was pretty cool but of course didn't have air conditioning. They had this 20 foot banner of the band with the 20th Anniversary logo and picture on it draped over the side of the building, pretty cool. That night we gave the Mexicans a good dose of sleazy rock as the crowd went nuts. It felt great as we tore through "Sex Action" and "Rip 'n Tear" to name a few as the crowd got wilder and wilder. The meet and greet lasted over an hour and a half and it felt great to play "South of the Border." The next day we were heading over to Guadalajara for another show. As we checked our luggage, sure enough we were overweight by a lot. We spaced that we would be flying on a small plane over to Guadalajara. The airline wanted to charge us over a grand! Once again that black cloud started forming over us. Gustavo the promoter decided he was going to drive the two big bins of merchandise eight hours from Monterrey to Guadalajara.

He really helped us out and literally showed up with the merch ten minutes before show time.

When we showed up at the airport we were met by a ton of fans! It's always exciting to have fans waiting for you at the airport. We signed a ton of stuff and took pictures with everybody. One guy had the entire Roxx Gang collection for me to sign. It was a great way to start off our day in Guadalajara. We fought crazy traffic all the way to the hotel. We stayed at this absolutely gorgeous Hilton. Of course we were turning every bloody head in that place. After we got checked in, we headed over to the club and sound checked on this stage that had to be at least 20 feet in the air. All I could think of was one wrong move in the dark and you'd be falling to your sheer death. We took some more pictures with fans afterwards and were showered with gifts. The promoters took us over to the Hard Rock for dinner. Now I've been to a ton of Hard Rocks but this had to be the nicest one I've ever seen. The steak I had for dinner was one of the best I ever had. Who would've thought? That night was a great show and a sweat fest for sure. The meet and great got a little scary. All we had between us and 500 rabid Mexican metal heads was a flimsy table. I got freaked out! Maybe it was jet lag, exhaustion, the heat but I panicked and flipped out on the security. All I could see was the table getting crushed and us suffocating. By the time we left the venue we were all fried. Riley was leaving at seven in the morning and Phil, Scotty, Jeff and I were going to stay an extra night at the Hilton. Ernesto the promoter asked if Scotty and I wanted to go out to an after hours club. We thought, "Hell, let's take it up a notch and do it." After we got changed we met Ernesto and his brother, Gustavo and Pepe in the lobby and headed over to a strip joint. It was a really nice place and we kicked back as they brought buckets of cold beer. Strip joints are all the same no matter where you go. All those chicks want to do is work your ass for money. By 5:30 I hit the wall and was ready to bolt. I settled back in my beautiful room and crashed hard. I woke around two in the afternoon and called Phil and met him out by the pool. Phil has actual videotape of me lounging on a sun chair from the 18th floor. You never know when you are being watched. Phil and I soaked up some sun as we waited forever for our drinks, meanwhile all these Mexican dudes were having buckets of beer brought to them every five minutes. It was hilarious watching Phil try to order a Blood Mary. The waiter was like "Que?" Phil responded "Bloody Mary" again "Que?" The more the waiter didn't understand the louder Phil got "BLOOODY FUCKIN MAAARY!!!" Needless to say our drinks never came. The more the day went by, all the travel and lack of sleep really started hitting me. Saturday night was pretty tame and Scotty, Jeff and I chilled in one of the Hilton bars. The place was dead and there was this Chinese guy who had been at the bar for a while and looked to be pretty hammered. Of course this nitwit came over to our table and started talking to us. He kept asking us where we were from and told Scotty that he didn't have a California accent and became more belligerent with every sentence. He kept getting closer to all of us and was pissing us off by the second. I finally told him sternly that if he didn't sit down I was going to knock his drunk ass out! I had had enough of this night and bolted back to my room. Our flight was at 8:30am which meant we had to leave the hotel at 6:30 in the morning. By the time we got home I was delirious and it had been one hell of a week.

As I recuperated over the next two weeks, my good old buddy Brian Majecinc was coming to L.A. for two and a half weeks. I was excited because I hadn't seen Brian in almost 18 years. Brian was friggin stoked because he hadn't been to L.A. since '88. A few months earlier Brian had put me in touch with an old friend of mine Paul Puz who I hadn't seen since '89 and unbeknownst to me was living right here in L.A. I arranged a night out with those guys the first night Brian got here and of course suggested to hit the Rainbow for dinner and drinks. I had Brian and Paul and his chick come over to my place for a drink. When they both got to my pad it was a fuckin trip. I hadn't seen these guys in almost 20 years. They were tripping because I basically looked exactly the same. However Brian and Paul looked a little different. They no longer had skin tight pants and cowboy boots. We had a riot that night hanging out and we were all in stitches over all those old stories of our old friends and the stupid shit we use to pull. Paul completely tripped my mind on so many things I forgot about. Paul is a drummer and I actually jammed with him when I was 15 with this guy who lived down the street from me who also attended the same private school as I did. Brain and I hung out quite a bit the next week and he decided to come to Vegas to see me and the Guns tear it up.

I was stoked that we were going back to Las Vegas and playing at the beautiful Sunset Station and Casino. These types of gigs were cake and a ton of fun. We flew in the day before the show and checked into the hotel. It was great to see the massive marquee outside the casino with our name on it and a huge digital picture of us. That afternoon, Steve and his wife Mary kicked it pool side with our own private cabana. It was a rare treat to see Steve lounging pool side. We had a great time that afternoon chilling, eating and drinking. That night good ole Lee had arranged a Limo for us and we were going to see Metal Skool at the Green River Valley Ranch Casino. Brian met me down in the lobby as we waited for Steve, Mary, Jeff and Lee to show up. Now for those of you who don't know who Metal Skool is, actually they are called Steel Panther now. They are a band that plays tribute to 80's metal with a lot of slapstick comedy in their set as well. These guys have the biggest draw in L.A. every Monday night in Hollywood at the Key Club and you can always bank on big celebrity sightings on those nights. Anyways, we got VIP'd for the show and Steve was excited to catch up with Ralph Saenz the singer who did a brief stint with L.A. Guns back in '97. We had a blast that night and Scott Ian from Anthrax was also in attendance. Steve and I went up and jammed with the guys and played "*Sex Action*". Next day we simply walked down to the casino and sound checked in the beautiful Madrid room. That night was fantastic and we packed the place. I thought it was one of the best shows of the year.

    The following week was one of the hardest and toughest

weekends to come. We had an east coast run in Connecticut, Pennsylvania and upstate New York. We were starting off in South Windsor which is just outside of Hartford.

We flew out of Burbank on Jet Blue into JFK which was a plus. Good ole Buffalo Bob stepped up once again and helped us out with a van. His buddy dropped the van off at JFK loaded with cold beers, sandwiches and snacks. Bob rules! An hour and a half later we rolled into Windsor. We were staying at some place called America's Best Value Inn and that says it all. We rolled up to the hotel and for sure it was an utter piece of shit. I think we were the first national band to play at this Club 645. The next day we slept in and all headed over to Denny's for a late breakfast. Once we started eating, Scott got a call on his cell phone. When he got off the phone he had this look of shock on his face. I said "what's up?" Scott said "Dude Traci Michealz from Peppermint Creeps is dead" We were all like "What?" Scott told us that Traci had died in his sleep in Dallas. I guess his band members went to wake him up and he was dead. I first met Traci about 8 years ago at the Rainbow when Lisa and I had come out to L.A. on vacation when we were still living in Florida. Traci instantly recognized me from Roxx Gang and engaged me in a long conversation about the band. Years later I got to know Traci and would always see him out and about. He was one of the nicest, self promoting, over the top rockers I had ever met.

The news of his death definitely put a damper on the day. The rest of the day was a complete cluster fuck and the club sucked.

Even though the place was packed we played like shit. The next day we headed over to Milton, PA. for an even worse night. Milton?????? This place was in the middle of nowhere. Now we were originally supposed to do this big outdoor thing called the Brash Bash, but I guess the promoter lost his land permit or something like that. He had passed the show onto this guy "Big Andy" who owned a club by the same name. The club was cool but it was in this tiny little town. That day was hot as hell and of course the air conditioning in my room wasn't working. That night sucked and it was fuckin dead. Big Andy turned into a Big Dick. We practically had to kiss his fat ass just to get the rest of our money. He actually told us that he was going to refund people's money and close up the bar. That was one of the stupidest things I've ever heard. The 50 or 60 people raised hell and I'm sure Big Andy did alright at the bar. Anytime the club owner is the soundman, it's a clear indication that he's a cheapskate. The next day we were heading up to Canandaigua, New York. My parents were actually driving down from Toronto to see me and come to the show. Bob put them up at the beautiful Inn on the Lake where we were staying. It was good to see my parents and we spent the afternoon together. That night was fun and my parents made it through the whole set and I even saw my dad rockin' out a few times. That night we partied in Scotty's suite and were still in shock over Traci's death.

    The next day we were coming home. Bob dropped us of at the Rochester airport and we were going to connect through JFK home into Burbank. As we got to the airport it looked like a nasty storm was brewing off in the distance. I had that sinking feeling, well I guess we all did of "looks like were not going home today." Sure enough, that's exactly what happened. A brutal storm rolled through New York State and basically crippled JFK and the surrounding areas. Our flight got delayed two hours then five and we were like "Well we might as well get the hell out of here, we're not going anywhere!" Everybody started getting shitty. I think we all started to take our frustrations out on each other especially when we found out the only way back home the next day was to leave at 6:30 am and fly into Long Beach! Bob once again came to our rescue. That man is a Saint! Bob booked us into the Crowne Plaza for the night and then rented us a Limo and took us to one of the best barbecue joints I have ever eaten at. If you are ever in Rochester, go check out Dinosaur Barbeque in downtown. After we munched on Cajun shrimp and ribs we headed back to the Plaza and I decided to go to bed since we had to get up at 4 am. The next day was a ball buster and by the time we got to Long Beach everyone was spent. Not only that, but we all had to make our own way back home. Scott and Phil actually took the subway home! Fortunately, Jeff's friend came and got him and me. That weekend really knocked the hell out of everybody. Take the good with the bad though.

    As Tuesday rolled around I prepared myself for Traci's funeral at the Hollywood Forever Cemetery. Mike Duda from WASP picked me up that afternoon and we headed over to the funeral while slamming a Bud Light tall boy. It was friggin hot as hell out and we parked the car at the cemetery and made our way into the funeral home. Traci had a huge turnout at his funeral. Phil and Scotty were also there. Mike and I grabbed one of the last two seats inside as the procession began. Once I realized I wasn't going to run into this crazy kid anymore it made me very sad as two tears rolled down my face. It really made me realize how precious life really is. The funeral lasted a little over an hour and it was pretty tough to get through it. Afterwards, Scotty, his girlfriend Kristin and I headed up to the Rainbow for a drink where we caught up with some other friends. It was a real draining day and so bloody hot.

The following week we were gearing up for the first annual Sunset Strip Music Festival. Basically it was a four day event celebrating the history of the Strip. We were asked to be part of it and we kicked off the first night with a headlining show at the Whisky. After we sound checked that Thursday we headed over to the House of Blues for a private party media event. Steve and I were the first to get there and started to do a ton of interviews as Phil and Scotty showed up. It was great to pose on the Red Carpet and always loved the sound of all those camera flashes. As we made our way into the House of Blues we saw Tommy Chong. I made small conversation with him and we all enjoyed the open bar. I think the highlight of the party was meeting and talking with Cheech Marin. I loved all those Cheech and Chong movies and Cheech was really cool and fun to talk with. Slash walked past me but I didn't say hello. He looked like he didn't want to be bothered.   Once again the Whisky kicked ass and was full of young, hungry rock n' rollers. As we were ending the set and ripping out the last power chord of "Rip 'n' Tear," I heard this tremendous crashing noise. Scott was going full on Pete Townsend to his bass and I guess pieces of it were flying all the way up to the balcony. A piece actually hit Phil's wife in the chest. As we were walking off stage I walked over demolished pieces of Scotty's Fender P-Bass. From what I hear he looked like a maniac destroying his instrument. Scotty's a total rock star. It was a great night and we had a fantastic time doing the meet and greet. For once we actually had time to hang with our fans at the Whisky.

Over the next two nights we attended two private parties. On Friday we headed over to the Standard hotel on Sunset for the "Virgin" party. Steve, Mary, Phil, Lisa and I kicked it pool side and enjoyed the open bar and snacked on various fancy finger foods. We shot the shit for hours and just kind of took it easy as Phil got more and more emaciated. During a few moments where the DJ stopped playing music and it was actually quiet for a change, Phil started yelling out S-T-A-C-E-Y B-L-A-D-E-S! more than a few times as everybody at the table cracked up. By 10'oclock the party pretty much wound down and we decided to head home. The next day at 4 pm was the press party at the London Hotel featuring a round table discussion with Larry King. Larry basically chatted with Mario and Lou Adler, the two big heavyweights of the Strip since the get go. It was pretty cool to watch and they had this big projector screen showing all old pictures of the strip from the 60's onward. After the press conference we all headed to the rooftop for drinks and dinner. It was a gorgeous day and the view on the rooftop was spectacular. The party soon cleared out as there was nowhere to sit down. It was a real pain in the ass trying to hold onto your drink and eat a plate of chicken and pasta while standing up. Steve, Mary, Scotty, Lisa and I waltzed over to the Bow for a few more drinks. Mary was a riot and it was funny watching her sip down these cosmopolitans the size of beach buckets. The next morning we had to get up at 4am to head over to LAX to catch a 6:30 am flight into Detroit. That night we were playing at the Stars and Stripes Festival. It was a bloody long day and by the time we got out of the airport, checked into the hotel, headed over to the concert grounds, checked out the gear, we were already baked. Not to mention none of us had anything to eat since the early morning! We were going on at 8pm and they drove us over to our dressing room to get ready with only 45 minutes to boot. We were all seeing spots with starvation. The show went well but we were all running on fumes. After the meet and greet, we demanded to be fed!!! They walked us over to this stand and said dive in. They actually made us eat vegetable shish-kabobs with stale rolls. It tasted like utter shit as I spit out what I had in my mouth. By that time we started to get a little agro. I mean c'mon people, get it fuckin together! This chick led us around the festival grounds while we were getting angrier by the minute in our sweaty stage clothes. We finally got to this one place and we sat down and finally ate crappy bar food. Of course we got bothered every bloody second by people while we were trying to eat. That shit always cracked me up. I wouldn't dream of doing that to someone while they were trying to eat their dinner. Now what topped this meal off was when we when we were leaving this guy comes up to the table and asks if we were done with everything. We said of course "yes". We assumed this guy worked there. In fact he was just some dude and dived right into all our leftovers. I clearly watched him go "All right!" as he dove into Riley's leftover salad and then proceeded to pick up my half eaten Rueben sandwich. I think all of us simultaneously went OOOHHHHHHH!!! It was one of the most disgusting things I've seen.

The following week we were leaving for two shows in Illinois. We flew into Chicago the day before July 4th. As we made our way to the luggage area I decided to have a cigarette outside while we waited for our bags. As I was chilling outside two cops come barreling out of the airport and made a b-line for me. The cops, one was a woman goes, "What's in your pockets, do you have identification on you!!" Then they started grabbing me and putting their hands in my pockets and I'm going "What the fuck is going on here!" At that point an airport employee comes out and goes "He went that way!" The cops look at me and go "Sorry." Sorry? These guys just gave me a heart attack! Later the woman cop came up to me and said "I'm sorry for that but you fit the description of someone trying to steal luggage. I said, "Well there is four of us that fit that description" and laughed. We drove a couple of hours to this shitty town called Freeport. Now playing on major holidays is either hit or miss. Of course this was definitely miss. We played outside in the back of a nightclub. The production and staging was great but it was dead! We were glad to get the hell out of Freeport and get over to Chicago. We were playing a big outdoor show that Saturday night and I just knew it was going to be a great night. We checked into the beautiful Hyatt Place. Before we headed over to the concert grounds, we did a quick photo shoot with the famous Gene Ambo and of course it turned out awesome. That night was fantastic and we kicked serious ass. I really felt it was one of the best shows of the year and there had to be at least 5000 people there. The MC for the event had asked us not to swear during the show. I assumed he was joking. He wasn't. Of course throughout the set we were like "How the fuck ya doing Chicago!" One of the MC's came up on stage with a hand written note that simply said "If you guys swear one more time, the cops are going to pull the plug and arrest you!" I looked over at side stage and saw an angry mob of cops and it looked like they had daggers for us. I started feeling like Jim Morrison for a second.

  That fall we finally went back to Europe after three long years. The tour was amazing and we sold out London at the famed Carling Academy and drew over eight hundred people in Dudley. We did the UK part of the tour with our mates Love/Hate which definitely helped the bill out. The tour also took us to Spain, Italy and Sweden. Now we did a vast amount of flying and there is always the chance that your shit may not show up when you have a connection. This notion bit me hard in the ass when we were flying from Vigo, Spain to Milan. We connected through Madrid and when we landed, nine of our pieces were missing. Of course we were playing that night. We had to wait for the next bloody flight to come. Now of course eight pieces showed up and guess which the ninth one didn't. My damn guitars! It would be the first time in my career that I played a show without my guitars. Fortunately some calls were made and a Les Paul was brought down for me. That guy really saved my ass that night. The rest of the tour was fantastic and it was so good to be in Sweden again. Those shows fuckin slayed and the gigs were packed with young hungry rockers.

At the end of the tour and we flew out of Stockholm and were to connect through London onto L.A. Of course rarely does shit go smoothly. Our flight out of Stockholm was a little delayed and we barely made our connection in London. Again we had that sinking feeling of our luggage and gear not showing up and sure enough when we landed at LAX, six of our pieces weren't there and again my guitars were missing. The next four days were hell and my guitars were missing. I talked to twenty different people at British Airways and got twenty different answers. That bloody airline is notorious for losing bags. I honestly thought my Cream Custom Les Paul and my Jackson Dinky were history. I really got depressed. Finally on the fourth night this guy from BA called me and said my axes were on the way to my place. "Thanks for shaving a few years off my life guys!"

A few months later, through and old friend in Florida, I got in touch with Roxx Gang bassist Roby Strine. It was so good to talk to him again and catch-up after 14 years! Roby is such a great guy and I was really good to laugh with him again and reminisce about old times. I'm really looking forward to seeing him in the near future at a Guns show.

Now I wasn't going to talk about this in the book but felt I needed to. For the last two years we have been fighting a war and that war is named Tracii Guns. Roughly two years ago Tracii had recruited the original drummer and singer of L.A. Guns before Phil and Steve joined the band. Tracii owns half the name so legally he is entitled to perform under that name and so the battle began. Tracii was also being booked by our old agents, how convenient! We didn't think this would have become such a problem but it really became a mud slinging war! Now what angered me the most is that this guy was not only affecting our band business wise but he was fucking with me and my band mates' livelihood! I never understood why he felt the need to do this to us especially after he was the one who quit the band! Not only have the "original members" come and gone, but Tracii now has put almost another new band together and is claiming he's the "real" L.A. Guns??????? Please! I could go on and on but I'm not going to.

The last five years have been absolutely great and chaotic at the same time. I really learned how to have a thick skin because people in this business certainly like to talk shit, especially on the internet. I have made some really good friends and some enemies to boot. From day one I had always wondered how the fans were going to react to me replacing Tracii. So far so good, but I will always be living in that dude's shadow and always be compared to him. He was such a big part of that band so there was really no way around it. I think that's why Jon Levin from Dokken and I are such good friends. We both replaced iconic guitar players in two big bands. It wouldn't plague him as much as it did me though. But he's a lot more neurotic than me and worried about too many other things, hahaha.

The Life of a Replacement Rock Star

Life in L.A. Guns has brought me many things I aspired to accomplish. I have been in tons of music magazines, have guitar, string and amp endorsements. I have traveled the world 5 times and have tons of adoring fans.

I honestly believe that life has a road mapped out for all of us. Those roads are full of bumps, dead ends, pot holes, left and right turns and forks. Rock and roll has given me a trial by fire so to speak. Looking back I wouldn't have changed a thing, well maybe I wouldn't have dated a few of those strippers. I thank God for keeping my eternal flame still burning to this day and not letting me give up, because all roads lead here.

THE END

80's Invasion Concert, Utah--- Summer '07

"Good night Cleveland!"

Made in the USA
Lexington, KY
06 May 2012